HEAVENLY HUMOR
for the
Grandmother's Soul

75 Bliss-Filled Inspirational Readings

BARBOUR
PUBLISHING

Contents

Section 10—Grandma's Medicine: Laughter

From Grandma's Kitchen:
Blessings

A grandma is a mom with extra frosting.

UNKNOWN

A Bakery Plus Love!

ANITA HIGMAN

*Whoever does not love does not
know God, because God is love.*
1 JOHN 4:8 NIV

What is it about grandmothers and sweet confections? When we go to Grandma's house, our sense of smell perks up right away. We burst through the kitchen door with nostrils flared, ready to breathe in all that sugar- and butter-laced air. And then comes the flavor. Our taste buds do sommersaults over Grandma's homemade nut breads, cookies, cobblers, cakes, and pies. But a grandmother's kitchen goes beyond good aesthetics—it's like a bakery plus love.

In my own young life growing up in Oklahoma, on many warm summer evenings after church, my parents would drive my brother and me to Grandmother Metzler's house, and we would sit on the glider, eating one of those sugary treats as the sunlight melted below the horizon like icing on a hot cake. We would relish those twilight hours as the temperatures cooled down and the lightning bugs started their twinkling. We visited while watching the fireflies, but I, no doubt, spent half the evening tripping after them, hoping to catch a few. At the time I had no idea magical memories were being created that would last a lifetime.

And part of the magic on those summer evenings was that each family member was given a bowl of Grandma's homemade cherry cobbler. She always made it from scratch with an extra cup of sugar poured on top, just to make certain it was sweet enough! You'll have to trust me on this one—it was sweet enough to make your lips curl into a gooey grin. It was delicious. Of course, Grandma always gave us a tall glass of iced tea to wash it down with. And go down it did. Just fine. I'm sure the bowls were always empty. And I don't think I have ever eaten finer cherry cobbler since those days at Grandma's house.

As an adult looking back, I realize those evenings weren't just about the delectable desserts at Grandma's house, but they were also about the love. The ingredients were mixed together and baked with care and the knowledge that her beloved grandchildren were going to enjoy every bite. Knowing her grandchildren would leave satisfied and just a little bit more content with life was a joy to Grandma. (And of course, knowing Grandma would be a little more loved was a joy, too!)

I can't help but see bits of God in that story. His world goes beyond good—it's creation plus love. What He created was for our delight. He made it with care, knowing that His beloved children were going to enjoy it all. He, too, wants to sit on the glider with us and visit with us and watch the fireflies in the twilight. He, too, wants us to feel satisfied and more at peace. He, too, wants us to know we are loved, and when we leave those twilight visits, He also hopes we will be more in love with Him!

Chicken 'n' Noodles

KATHY DOUGLAS

*"Stand at the crossroads and look; ask for the ancient paths,
ask where the good way is, and walk in it,
and you will find rest for your souls."*
JEREMIAH 6:16 NIV

Grandma Halstead did some things just like her mother, Nellie Bell. And yes, that was my poor great-grandma's real name.

My mom tells me both farm women, who made their noodles from scratch, would make up the dough then drape it over dish towels hung on the backs of kitchen chairs. That gave the dough time to dry out or puff up or do *something* before the final rolling out and cutting. Grandma Bell and Grandma Halstead did their noodles the same way. When it came to preparing the chicken for their chicken 'n' noodles, however, these two farmers' wives parted company.

My own mother, who never slaughtered a chicken herself, found the grandmas' procedures neat and orderly. She watched her mother do it many times over. Grandma Mildred Halstead went out and chose the unfortunate bird from their flock. She'd carry it by the scruff of its neck to the chopping block. She put one foot on the chicken's head, held its feet with her free hand, and with a quick swipe of the sharpened butcher knife in her right hand, the chicken was ready to make his or her contribution to the 'n' noodles.

Grandma's meticulous style impressed my mom as a young girl. Some of their neighbors hung their headless chickens on the clothesline and. . .well, TMI (too much information) as grandkids today say. Suffice it to say, Grandmas Bell and Halstead's simplicity lacked the spectacle and the barbarism of their neighbors. Me? I never witnessed any of the above. But I never messed with my grandmas either.

From there the grandmas' chicken preparations differed. Nellie plucked her chickens for roasting. A bit squeamish, Mildred couldn't "abide," as she would say, chicken skin. She skinned her chickens before cooking.

Fast forward to the distant future.

In one of my favorite sci-fi television episodes set in the twenty-fifth century, one of the characters was horrified when her husband recounted his mother's meat preparation. The character, whose food came already prepared from a machine called a "replicator," stood horrified.

"Your mother touched *raw meat*? With her *hands*?"

Today most of us live somewhere between the chopping block and a replicator. We may anticipate the coming of new appliances like replicators, and we want nothing to do with the old days of slaughtering our own chickens.

Do we take that attitude with the Old Testament scriptures? I've heard women say, "I'd just rather study the New Testament," or "I find the Old Testament too hard to understand."

The Old Testament deepens our appreciation and understanding of the New Testament scriptures. Jesus said, "These are the very Scriptures that testify about me" (John 5:39 NIV). "The ancient paths" lay down for us all that is to come in both the New Testament and the future. I'm going to keep digging in and studying those foundational words.

As for chicken? I'll eagerly wait for replicators. And—in the meantime—I'll stick with my pre-slaughtered, prepackaged, boneless, *skinless* chicken.

Chicken Foot Soup

KATHY DOUGLAS

I remember the days of long ago; I meditate on all your
works and consider what your hands have done.

PSALM 143:5 NIV

With three-year-old Erica in tow, Anna and her husband went back to "the old country," Hungary, in 1985. With an independent streak that would eventually repeat itself in her own grown daughters, Anna left Hungary as a young teenager to start a new life for herself in the United States. There she met her husband, established a career, and started her own family. Now she was ready to take her firstborn back to her roots. It was time for daughter Erica to meet her Hungarian grandparents.

Big-eyed and overwhelmed by the strange language and customs, Erica was eagerly and lovingly received by her extended family in Hungary. On their first Sunday in Hungary, her poor but hospitable grandparents invited all the family for a traditional Sunday dinner. That meant the weekly treat: meat as the main course. The first course, however, was the soup.

Erica's *nagymama* (pronounced "nudgemama") set the pot in the middle of the table. Erica looked in the pot; the color drained from her face.

"What's *that,* Mommy?"

Like a misplaced bone from a horror movie, a chicken foot floated—complete with its talons—in the soup.

"The chicken foot is for good luck," Anna explained to her wide-eyed toddler.

Erica did eat some of the soup, but she made sure the talon-toed chicken leg didn't make it into her bowl—no matter how much luck came with it.

"We used to use everything on the chicken," Anna said, relating the story with a laugh and her rich accent. "When I was a kid growing up in Hungary, my sister and I used to fight over who got to cut up which part of the chicken. I remember fighting over a chicken brain with my sister." She paused. "My mom could feed our family of six with one scrawny chicken for five or six meals. Funny. . .I had forgotten about all this until you asked."

Do we remember the things we should remember? Do we put behind us the things we need to forget? The Bible tells us there are things to be remembered and things best forgotten. Peter wanted to make sure those he instructed in the faith remembered all he taught them (2 Peter 1:15 NIV). Paul says, "Remember Jesus Christ, raised from the dead, descended from David" (2 Timothy 2:8 NIV).

Yet Paul made it clear that sometimes it's best to forget things.

We don't get everything right, and others don't always either. Costly mistakes hurt. Yet carrying around such baggage doesn't help us get on with the job of living. Paul encourages us to move on. "[I'm] forgetting the past," he wrote, "and looking forward to what lies ahead" (Philippians 3:13 NLT).

Erica never forgot the chicken foot soup. As a college freshman, she and her classmates had to write a story about their personal cultural backgrounds. Erica entitled her paper "Chicken Foot Soup for the Cultured Soul," and wouldn't you know it? . . . She got an A.

Grandma's After-Dinner Directive

TINA KRAUSE

*They broke bread in their homes and
ate together with glad and sincere hearts.*
ACTS 2:46 NIV

My paternal grandmother was a no-nonsense woman. Raising four sons alone, she demanded obedience and respect, and Lord help the person who challenged her!

Grandma's frequently repeated directives were her trademark. A perfectionist, she was intolerant of disorganization and often quoted the phrase "There's a place for everything and everything in its place!" whenever a family member struggled to find something.

But my personal favorite—a directive I've embraced as my own—resounded at the conclusion of every meal. As the men loosened their belts and migrated to the living room, she'd announce, "I wasn't the only one who ate dinner, you know." Grandma expected everyone—men included—to help clean up.

As a self-proclaimed kitchen evader (and too often an *in*vader), the mother of two adult children, and grandmother of five, I now spend as little time in the kitchen as possible. After all, I've already served most of my life in the mess hall and I'm ready for transfer to a different unit; or at least a promotion from the galley to above-deck duties.

Unlike men, women are expected to cook and clean. I realize this practice dates back to biblical times, but must I enjoy it? Samuel warned the people in the Old Testament what would happen if they insisted on having a king rule them. "He will take your daughters from you and force them to cook and bake." Note the word *force*. Yet I've noticed that the younger female generation rejects the *you-woman-you-cook* concept.

Years ago whenever out-of-town relatives visited, we would gather at my parents' home for family dinner. Mom, who gladly accepted kitchen duty as her lot in life, served a huge meal as always. After-ward, the men moseyed to the couch and recliners to watch television while the women cleared the table. Mom jumped up (she hardly sat down during dinner) and forged into the kitchen, balancing plates and bowls in both hands. I helped, while the younger women dispersed in the same direction as the men.

Instantly my grandmother's words spewed from my mouth to un-suspecting ears, "Excuse me, but the older women weren't the only ones who ate dinner, you know." As the young ladies filed into the kitchen, the men stayed glued to their positions of immunity. Sud-denly out of his seat of comfort my father spoke. "You know what my mother always said," he stated flatly. "If you ate, you help clean up!"

Was my imagination running away with me? Did Dad just convey grandma's directive from his cushy portal of self-exemption? I could have sworn he ate, too.

Yes, my paternal grandma was decades ahead of her time. And now as a bona fide grandma myself, I've acquired her no-nonsense approach. So here's how I see it. Although a man is king of his castle, he should still clean up the mess he helped create. Either that or I'm using the mess hall for above-deck duties only. I've been promoted.

Unless, of course, I ate dinner, too.

South of the Border

JEAN FISCHER

For all have sinned and fall short of the glory of God.
ROMANS 3:23 NIV

From the Great Depression until 1967, Wisconsin banned yellow-colored oleo-margarine—not plain oleo, just the yellow kind. Oleo's overall advantages were that it was cheaper than butter, and it stored better. On the downside, unless yellow coloring was added, oleo looked greasy and white, like lard. Yellow oleo became wildly popular among consumers, yet in The Dairy State the "yellow stuff" was viewed as a demon that threatened to put dairy farmers out of business. This left Wisconsin residents with a dilemma. They could live without their yellow oleo, or smuggle it into the state.

Grandma smuggled it. My parents did, too, and I'm ashamed to admit that I helped them. In the 1950s, when I was just a child, I had already been sucked into the Oleo Wars—and at the hands of my Christian family!

We lived near the Wisconsin–Illinois border, and in Illinois oleo was as legal as butter. Day and night, carloads of dairy-state oleo smugglers crossed south over the border to snatch their portion of golden fat. Grandmothers did it. So did stay-at-home moms, spinster aunts, and (horrors!) even the pastor of our church!

My family's method of smuggling never wavered. At dusk, Grandma loaded a blanket into the back seat of our car. We all settled into our big Buick with Dad acting as the getaway driver and Mom, Grandma, and me pretending to be a "nice" little family out for a twilight drive. We steered clear of the main highway and traveled the back roads to the border. Our hearts thumped hard as we crossed the imaginary line into Zion, Illinois. There, at Packy's Place, a tiny grocery store attached to an AA Club, Grandma purchased a half dozen pounds of yellow oleo. She stuffed it into a shopping bag along with a few other items that she bought to hide "the evidence." Meanwhile, Mom, Dad, and I waited in the car, the engine running, worried that our Wisconsin license plates might give us away. Finally, and almost too casually, Grandma strolled out of the store and slipped into the back seat next to me. She plopped the shopping bag onto my lap, covered my legs with the blanket, and off we drove into the darkness toward the state line. I couldn't help but worry that the oleo police might get us, and I didn't rest until I was safe at home and the contraband yellow stuff was safely stored away, hidden in the back of the refrigerator.

Grandma confessed to me years later that she felt guilty about breaking the law, even if it was only to buy oleo. It may have been just a "little sin," but Grandma pointed out to me that in God's eyes, sin is sin. The Bible says in 1 John 1:9 that if we confess our sins, God is faithful and just to forgive us and cleanse us from all unrighteousness. I'm certain that Grandma confessed her oleo sin to God. . .and now, I think I will, too.

A Ham Salad Christmas

JEAN FISCHER

Do not neglect to do good and to share what you have,
for such sacrifices are pleasing to God.
HEBREWS 13:16 ESV

Mom always served ham salad sandwiches on Christmas Eve. As a kid, I hated eating ham salad when my friends' families were having roast turkey dinners with all the trimmings. I felt embarrassed by our Christmas Eve suppers. Certainly we could afford something better.

"Whoever heard of ham salad for Christmas?" I complained.

"It's a tradition," Mom answered. "One that Grandma started when I was a little girl."

I put up with her tradition until after Grandma passed away. Then when Mom continued to serve the sandwiches, I went on strike. I vowed that I'd never eat another ham salad sandwich. Instead I suffered through Christmas Eve eating anything else that was on the table:

potato chips, pickles, and even fruitcake. (You know things are bad when the best choice is fruitcake.)

I grew up and moved away. Still, every Christmas Eve, I went home to celebrate with Mom and Dad, and I continued to resist those awful sandwiches.

Then, one year, when I got there, I smelled turkey roasting. "Turkey!" I exclaimed. "We're having turkey?"

"Just for you," Mom answered. "I'm starting a new tradition."

I celebrated that I could end my strike and eat what "normal" people ate on Christmas Eve. Then as I helped Mom with dinner, I asked, "So why did we always have ham salad sandwiches?"

"Well," Mom began, "there was one Christmas when my family was very poor. We lived in a rented house near the railroad tracks, and freight trains traveled that line connecting Chicago and Milwaukee. Bums rode in the boxcars."

"Stowaways," I interrupted, wanting to be politically correct.

She continued, "Around suppertime that Christmas Eve, the doorbell rang, and when Grandpa answered it, he found a hobo standing on our front porch. The man was dirty and cold, and he asked if he could have something to eat. Grandma had just made ham salad for supper. It was the best meal that our family could afford. She ground up some ham with a hand-cranked meat grinder. Then she added mayonnaise, a little pickle relish, and a good dash of pepper. She was just spreading it on slices of homemade bread when the man rang the bell. Grandma didn't want anybody to go hungry, so she packed a brown paper sack with our sandwiches and gave it to him. I'll never forget how that man smiled when Grandma handed him our supper. After that, in better times, we always made ham salad sandwiches on Christmas Eve to remind us that other people had nothing to eat."

After hearing Mom's story, I wasn't so eager for a turkey dinner with all the trimmings. I wished that we were having ham salad so I could savor the tradition. Finally I understood what I had missed all those years. Grandma's ham salad had been a blessing. The proof is in the Bible in Proverbs 22:9: "The generous will themselves be blessed, for they share their food with the poor" (NIV).

Getting a Grip

JO UPTON

Don't just listen to the word.
You fool yourselves if you do that.
You must do what it says.

JAMES 1:22 NIrV

Super Bowl! For most folks, these two words immediately bring to mind one of the year's major sporting events. During the last Super Bowl, our home was filled with laughter and conversation among the family and friends we had invited to watch the big game. With plenty to eat and drink, our guests were soon filling plates and glasses and heading toward the room with the largest TV.

The youngest member of the party, my two-year-old grand-daughter, Leila, was creating her own amusement. During the game, she played with toys and ran from spot to spot visiting with everyone. All this activity had apparently made Leila quite thirsty, and all the unguarded drinks sitting around were almost too much for her to ignore. As she entered the TV area, Leila soon noticed that several of the teen guests were talking, paying no attention to their food. . .or to her. Being a self-sufficient little girl, she looked around and found a cup within reach that was filled with a cool drink. She picked it up and started to take a sip, but her dad—my son Matt—was watching. He cautioned her to put the cup down before it spilled and to leave the drinks alone. Leila was provided with her own drink and went back to the toys. At first this seemed to work.

But when her thirst returned, so did Leila. Entering the room, she found that once again there were plenty of unattended drinks to choose from. Just as she made her choice, Matt realized what she was about to do. Turning toward her now outstretched arms, he said, "Don't touch that cup." Leila, recognizing her father's voice, immediately placed the cup back on the table and her arms to her side. Thinking it was over, we watched with smiles as she bent down, placed her little face directly over the cup, and tried to lap it out, never again touching the cup! She had, at least in theory, done exactly as her dad had asked, but still managed to get a taste of the forbidden cola.

Of course the drink was taken from Leila, and she was given something more age-appropriate. Everyone laughed at the way a small child reasons and the party continued. But how often do we, as adults, listen to our heavenly Father and fool ourselves into believing we have "obeyed," when in truth we have only "heard"?

Often we read the Bible as just another book, stopping short when it comes to applying the verses to our day-to-day problems and decisions. We recognize our Father's voice, but we don't fully apply His instructions.

God's desire is to direct, protect, and guide us through His Word, but none of it works if we aren't committed to doing fully what He intended. When we finally understand the importance of hearing with our spirits as well as our ears, we begin to respond like maturing Christians. . .instead of thirsty children!

Cookies, Coffee, and Scrabble

SHELLEY R. LEE

May our Lord Jesus Christ himself and God our Father,
who loved us and by his grace gave us eternal encouragement and good hope,
encourage your hearts and strengthen you in every good deed and word.
2 THESSALONIANS 2:16–17 NIV

I loved time with just Grandma and me. Long before I loved coffee, its rich aroma wafted from her warm, yellow kitchen. I wanted to like coffee so much. Milk in a mug was working for me, though, and it would for years to come. And somehow milk tasted better in those sturdy Ford Company cups from Grandma's cupboard anyway.

From another room you could hear the distinct squeak of her pulling open the cupboard doors layered with coats of glossy paint. Swung open, the contents of endearing dishes and yellow striped juice glasses smiled at me.

There were many things I loved about being at Grandma and Grandpa's house, but Scrabble and cookie time had to be the best. When Grandpa was settled in bed, always early in the evening, Grandma would set me up with a leisurely bath. Once in my comfy pajamas, I would meander into the kitchen, lit only by a sink light and a small wall sconce near the yellow and chrome table. Grandma would be at the counter tidying up dishes and things. "Sit down, honey," she would say, and then she'd ask if I wanted something as she reached into the high cupboard next to the old Frigidaire. At my request, she pulled out the chunky vanilla sandwich cookies that she kept double wrapped for freshness, like she did most things.

Dunked in the milk in the Ford Company cup, those cookies had no rival. She would usually stop me at three cookies. Four was a real treat and required a reopening of the double wrapping, but Grandma seemed to enjoy every second, sort of giggling under her breath.

Cookies and milk complete, it was time to break out the Scrabble game. The tattered corners of the box always got me thinking about all the games that were played on that board. All the words and the waiting as the plastic clock ticked on the wall. All the special rules Grandma would make. Some were standing rules like always get eight tiles instead of the regulation seven (so luxurious!). Other rules were created as we went along. "Honey, you can just trade in some of those letters. . .that's not right, here let's take care of that," she would say, letting me walk all over the rules with no guilt at all. All for the sake of encouraging me in the game, she'd let me win almost every time, until I got much older anyway. She had amazing skill at the game but would play a three-letter word or leave a spot open so I could use my Q. When I'd play a triple word that she set me up for, she'd say,

"Wow, you're getting good!"

Today as I take in the fresh aroma of coffee that beckons me to my kitchen for a cup of delectable brew, it is inseparable from thoughts of Scrabble, and yellow, and Grandma giggling and encouraging me.

Going to Grandma's House:
Character

One hundred years from now it will not matter
what kind of house I lived in, how much money I had,
or what my clothes were like. But the world may be a
little better because I was important in the life of a child.

UNKNOWN

My Jam-Covered Face

ANITA HIGMAN

His mercy extends to those who fear him,
from generation to generation.
LUKE 1:50 NIV

My grandmother Metzler was all things soft. She always wore the same delicate fragrance, which I now associate with her. Years after she passed away, I would sometimes stop by the fragrance counter at one of my favorite department stores just to take a whiff of my grandmother's perfume. The store would always have a display bottle for a free sample, and I'd give my wrist a spray of the dark liquid. For a lovely moment or two, it brought back the memory of her. Always delightful.

My dear grandmother also wore soft gloves and a fur stole around her shoulders when she dressed up. She looked so pretty and yes, so soft! Knowing the nature of kids, I pray my mouth wasn't covered with jam as I buried my cheeks in that fur. But to a child, that velvety shawl was irresistible.

Even the inside of my grandmother's purse had a soft, powdery scent, and I loved to turn the little brass snaps, open it up, and breathe in the smell. Little do grandmothers know that their grandchildren notice everything, even the smallest things that might appear insignificant. Kids come in small packages, so they tend to take in what is minuscule, which is probably why they come home with so many beetles and bugs! But those same qualities help children to cultivate a sense of curiosity and wonder. Just like the way I marveled at my grandmother's softness. For me that velvety quality that surrounded my grandmother was welcoming, and it made me want to be near her. It made her even more lovable.

As an adult, when I think of my grandmother's softness, the first word that comes to mind is *mercy*. What a blessed word—*mercy*—which is like a gentleness of spirit. My grandmother had plenty of gentleness as well, and I'm sure I was in frequent need of it. Grandma was merciful every time I came close to breaking a treasure, or I begged for more candy, or I put on a sourpuss face when I lost a game of dominoes.

I'm so glad my heavenly Father is not only a God of justice but also a God of mercy. And that His mercy is so pleasant and welcoming it makes me want to be near Him. His mercy is so enduring, so alluring. It is a light we are attracted to since we are used to wandering in the darkness of our failings. It is the compassion and clemency that our souls crave!

Thank You, God, for Your gentleness of spirit when we deliberately smear our jam-covered faces into Your goodness. Every time we come close to breaking Your human treasures, every time we beg for more when we have forgotten to thank You for what we have, and every time we grumble and put on a sourpuss face when we don't like the answers to our prayers. Thank You for that blessed word *mercy*!

Gutsy Grandmas

KATHY DOUGLAS

One day Ruth's mother-in-law Naomi said to her, "My daughter,
I must find a home for you, where you will be well provided for."
RUTH 3:1 NIV

Gutsy grandmas make their families proud. Sometimes they make their family members nervous or even scare them half to death. Yet most of us gladly give our gutsy grandmas kudos and a hearty thumbs-up.

Ella Tuttle Mattheson started her second career—as a newspaper columnist—when she was 100. As a well-established columnist at age 102, she shooed her interviewer out of her apartment. "I'd appreciate it," she told him, "if you'd hurry up and take whatever pictures you need. I'm on a deadline for this Thursday's edition." The interviewer hurried up—and out!

Sixty-five-year-old Texas grandmother Val Renfro took off in pursuit of a purse snatcher after he reached inside her car, grabbed her purse, and started running. Fortunately this smart grandma doesn't keep her cell phone in her purse. Val reached into her bra, where she does keep her phone, and called the police. With the help of bystanders, she stopped the thief even before police arrived.

Not all grandmas can chase down purse snatchers or become newspaper columnists at one hundred. For some, their gutsiness shows itself in retaining a joyful spirit in spite of ailing bodies. They reach out to others in prayer, by telephone calls, or by cards. My own mother, who is a great-great-grandma, never fails to send birthday cards to every one of her family and dozens of friends. She moved closer to us "kids" when she was over eighty. She began attending our church since the one she had attended for over fifty years was too distant. She has become the favorite—and possibly the oldest—member of her Sunday school class. Most of the fortysomethings in her class have an eagerness to partake of her wisdom. Mom didn't start a new career after retirement, and she certainly couldn't chase down a purse snatcher if she had to. . . . I don't think. But she's as gutsy as they come. She does what she can do with God's daily grace.

A few gutsy grandmas show up in the scriptures, too. Ruth's mother-in-law, Naomi, showed herself resilient even before her first grandson was born. Ruth did everything her late husband's mother told her to do. The young widow was rewarded with a (second) good husband, a home of her own, and eventually a son.

Grandma Naomi didn't quietly bow out of Ruth's life when the nuptials ended. When her grandson arrived, "Naomi took the child in her arms and cared for him" (Ruth 4:16 NIV). In a time and culture when women were often secondary citizens, Naomi got things done—

her way. Just like some gutsy grandmas of today.

As for that grandma who chased down the purse snatcher? When she saw him at the police station, he apologized. Gutsy Val was neither grudging nor vindictive. Holding her purse close to her side, her cell phone tucked safely back in its usual place, she dismissed the thief with five words.

"Apology accepted," she said. "God bless you."

Follow the Leader

LINDA HOLLOWAY

Therefore I urge you to imitate me.
1 CORINTHIANS 4:16 NIV

I'm taking the checkbook back to the office," I said to my husband, Jerry.

Silence from behind the newspaper. I walked to his easy chair and thumped the paper's fold. "Josh is playing with his cars in the kitchen."

He tipped back his head and said, "Huh? Okay."

"I'll be back down in a couple of minutes."

I knew Jerry heard me. When we'd made eye contact, he nodded. However, the paper immediately hid his face. Not a good sign for attention to our two-and-a-half-year-old grandson. *I'll hurry. Josh probably won't miss me.*

As I climbed the stairs, I remembered Josh tumbling down those steps two months earlier. He screamed. Then I screamed and rushed to him. Thankfully, double-padded carpet cushioned his fall so he wasn't hurt. For a month he'd held the railing spindles and negotiated the steps better. *What is it about stairs and toddlers?*

At the door of our office, which contained our computer, library, and the cat's litter box, I stepped over the baby gate. As I reached the desk, I heard Jerry yell, "Where are you, Josh?"

I turned toward the hall muttering, "He lost him. In less than two minutes, he lost him." Then I experienced one of those "Gee, I wish I had a camera" moments. Josh raised his foot toward the top of the gate and stretched his leg. He frowned and pressed his lips together. Finally he stared up at me with raised eyebrows, open mouth, and foot mid-air, short of his goal.

Jerry appeared beside him and caught the mini-drama. We both burst into laughter. Josh dropped his foot to the floor and cocked his head. Jerry said, "I guess he doesn't understand why you could get over the gate but he can't."

Josh looked at him. . .then at me. Next he put both hands on top of the gate and gazed past me into the office. So much to explore.

"Come on, little guy," said Jerry, picking him up. Tears welled in Josh's eyes. Josh cried out and reached toward me. Jerry bounced him and said, "Let's go play with your cars. Grandma'll be down in a few minutes."

At the word "cars" the tears stopped. Immediately Josh snaked one arm around Grandpa's neck and grinned. "Green one," he said.

Still chuckling, I returned the checkbook to its home in the top desk drawer. I had no idea that Josh was nearby and would try to follow me. The sight of Josh's leg strained to its limit and his obvious bewilderment. . .priceless.

In our lives little eyes watch, ears hear, and hearts absorb more than we know. Can we say to our grandchildren, as Paul said to the Corinthians, "Imitate me"? A few verses later Paul advises us how to be good leaders: "Follow my example, as I follow the example of Christ" (1 Corinthians 11:1 NIV).

I'm Going Home

SHELLEY R. LEE

Listen to advice and accept discipline,
and at the end you will be counted among the wise.
PROVERBS 19:20 NIV

When Dexter was three years old, he and his three older brothers were staying with Grandma and Grandpa for a couple days. At lunchtime Grandma Gloria had frozen yogurt pops and a piece of candy for each of them if they ate all their lunch. But Dexter did not want to eat all his lunch. Grandma conceded to give him the yogurt pop but not the candy. He liked the yogurt and asked for another. He was denied his request unless he finished his lunch, and then he could have more yogurt, and the piece of candy.

Fair enough, thought Grandma. Dexter, however, stomped off, displeased to say the least. But he seemed settled enough when he joined in play and cartoons with his brothers downstairs. So Grandma headed up the stairs to work in the backyard for a little while.

As she tended to her flowers, movement caught her eye through the windows into the kitchen and she saw the entire scene. Dexter pushed a stool next to the refrigerator, where he proceeded to climb up and get the candy he wanted. He wiggled down off the stool then, opened the freezer drawer, and found the second yogurt he was wanting as well.

When Grandma stepped inside to tell him he could not have those things now, but he could have them later with dinner, he was very upset. "I'm leaving!" he said. He stomped out of the room again. A few minutes later his brothers came upstairs, and Grandma heard the front door shut. "Who's going outside?" she asked.

They all walked to the front door and out to the porch. There, heading down the driveway, was little Dexter with his suitcase in hand. He could not have the food he wanted, so he was going home. In his young mind and limited understanding, he just wanted out of his situation, and of course that's about as far as he thought. Grandma was there to talk him back into the house, even though he wasn't very happy and couldn't have his treats yet.

It's so funny, the things the grandchildren say and do. It's easy to think that they are just, well, children, and that as an adult I am not so prone to such blunders. Then a verse like Proverbs 19:20 thunks me upside the head. I realize the many times I was not as mature as perhaps I would have liked to have been. To be fair, my understanding is often limited. But to be honest, it's much easier to walk away in a huff than to accept the discipline and wait a little while for the treats.

Joining the Dance

JANICE HANNA

And David danced before the LORD with
all his might, wearing a priestly garment.
2 SAMUEL 6:14 NLT

For weeks I'd been filling my granddaughter's head with stories about how great my upcoming play was going to be. I could hardly wait for the precocious two-year-old to see it. As the show's writer and director, I was especially proud of the actors, singers, dancers, costumes, and so on. I also knew that Peyton would enjoy the childlike story of "Zaney Muldaney"—a girl on a journey to Kingdom Come. I could almost picture her response.

Finally the day came. Peyton arrived at the theater with her mommy. She was dressed to the nines and so hyped up we could barely get her calmed down to sit next to me. I settled into my chair in the auditorium, the excited toddler bouncing up and down in her seat to my left. She released a gasp as the curtain opened and the actors, singers, and dancers kicked off the show with great animation. Peyton turned to me, eyes wide, clearly mesmerized. I knew right away she was hooked, but how would she handle sitting still for two hours?

Thank goodness that darling little girl had the time of her life. She watched, in rapt awe, as the performance carried on. The music seemed to captivate her. So did the acting and the costumes. More than anything, though, she loved the dancers, particularly the ballerinas. Every time they came onto the stage, her little face lit up and she began to squeal with delight.

As the show came to an end, however, Peyton's countenance changed. In fact, as the on-stage dancers began their final number, Peyton began to cry. When we asked her why, she responded—through her tears—"They never asked *me* to come up on the stage and dance with them."

Ouch! My little darling felt left out. I certainly hadn't planned for that. But yet, there it was. Peyton wanted her shot on the stage but didn't get it.

Watching her dramatic reaction made me think of something else, too. How often do we feel like Peyton? We watch others joyously dance and wonder if we'll ever get our shot.

There's good news today! God calls each of us to join Him in the dance of life. When we become His partner, we share in the joy of the journey. How does this play out? We "join in"—at church, in various ministries, in relationships with others. Simply put, we fill our dance card. He leads the way, showing us the right steps, and we join Him, a willing partner to His leading.

Now *there's* a dance we can all enjoy!

Non-Stop Talker

JANICE HANNA

In the same way, the Spirit helps us in our weakness.
We do not know what we ought to pray for,
but the Spirit himself intercedes for us through wordless groans.
ROMANS 8:26 NIV

It happens every time I put one of my granddaughters into the car seat behind the driver's seat in my car. It's as if putting them into that little chair flips some sort of switch. . .a switch that says, "Let the talking begin!"

On and on and on they go, chattering about thousands of nonsensical things as I do my best to split my focus between driving and responding to their never-ending (and often goofy) questions. Sometimes they will repeat things, sure I haven't heard them the first twelve times. I do my best to respond, but making sense of the conversation is difficult at best, especially when I'm driving in traffic.

Sometimes I turn on the radio, or perhaps their favorite CD, hoping they'll take the hint. In the end, I usually end up turning the music off. Why? Because the talking continues, louder than before. It's tough enough to deal with the chattering. Add music to the mix and my focus on the road goes out the window.

Perhaps you can relate. Maybe you have a little one who thrives on conversation. If so, you've likely developed tactics for how to best deal with the ongoing chatter while driving. Hopefully your methods are better than mine, especially when the nonsensical talking kicks in or the questions grow repetitive.

As I think about the conversations I have with the toddlers in my life, I'm reminded of my prayer time with the Lord. I find myself repeating things, wondering if He heard me the first twelve times. Instead of a focused, well-thought-out conversation, I ramble, much of the conversation about myself, not Him. That's why I'm so thrilled that the Holy Spirit actually helps us in our prayer time. When we don't know what to say—or what to pray—He intercedes for us, making sense of it all.

Thank goodness God is more patient than this frazzled grandma. He doesn't turn up the radio to drown out my chattering. In fact I have His undivided attention. He leans in closer than before, listening carefully, and even helps me make sense of my heart's cry, responding with such grace that I can't help but feel loved. And special.

Oh, that I will have the patience to do the same when those little granddaughters of mine are seated behind me as I drive down the road! Heaven help me.

A Grandmother of Grit

VALORIE QUESENBERRY

Strength and honour are her clothing;
and she shall rejoice in time to come.

PROVERBS 31:25 KJV

I learned about grit from my grandmother. I'm not talking about the kind you eat or the type you sweep off the porch. I'm referring to the inner steel that takes a woman through life, in spite of the odds.

My maternal grandmother knew all about the ebb and flow of life. Growing up on a dirt farm in Missouri, raised in the era of the Depression, she was acquainted with hardship and hard work. I've heard the stories of her childhood that bespoke the difficulties of those times. She'd recall how she and her siblings carried biscuits and jelly in a syrup can to school and traded with other children for their lunch of corn bread and milk. She'd tell me about the simple fun she had rolling in sawdust piles and then jumping into the creek. She'd smile as she told about the little friend whose clothing "faded black" (with dirt). She'd tell stories about hiding from stampeding cattle, eating green apples in the orchard, riding a billy goat, and killing snakes. She'd relate the hard, meager existence that was all she'd ever known until her move to St. Louis as a teenager. She'd talk about the difficult days she'd seen as a wife and mother—trying to feed a family of ten on a small salary, keeping up with the daily routine of housework, worrying about the future of her family. She came up with creative ways to supplement my grandfather's wages—taking in ironing, reselling produce, making and marketing homemade popsicles and peanut brittle. She gardened and canned. She knew how to stretch ingredients and make them taste good. She lived with little, and went on anyway. She had grit.

Yet I also learned about grace from her. She didn't blame God for her troubles; she didn't become bitter. She bumped along with the tide of life and became a better person because of it. She even found bits of humor in the hardship. She'd chuckle about the homespun fun of her early years; she'd recall life's lessons with a sweet smile.

I do know that it made her frugal; my grandma never wasted anything. Whether it was using a potato peeler rather than a knife (to save more of the potato) or rinsing out plastic wrap (to be reused), she was careful to conserve. It left her grateful; she was thankful for all the blessings of life. It gave her depth; she was not a "will-o-the-wisp" type, but a steady, dependable woman.

My life has been different from hers, but I've benefitted from her wealth of wisdom. My grandma was beautiful as a young woman, but the beauty of her mature soul was also exceedingly lovely. And that's what a woman with real grit is—beauty deep inside that sees you through with a smile.

If I Were in Charge

MARCIA HORNOK

Among the inhabitants of the earth. No one can restrain
His hand or say to Him, "What have You done?"
DANIEL 4:35 NKJV

"I could be president someday," Xander said.

"Yes, you could," I answered. "What would you do if you were president of the United States?"

Xander had recently turned seven, and I wondered what he would say.

"I would not let any dirty cars park next to clean cars."

"What else?"

"I would make old people live in old houses and young people live in"—he fumbled for the right word—"new houses."

"Where would I have to live?"

"You're an old person," he said, as if I should know that.

"Okay, what else would you do as president?"

"You could only kill one deer in your life, but you could kill all the animals that kill deer." After a while he added, "And every Tuesday would be a no-school day."

Xander is ten now. Recently I reminded him of his presidential aspirations and asked if he had any new ideas about what he would do in that position.

He said, "I would make the Sunday funnies funnier—Garfield for Governor!" Then he added, "When a person has an idea he can write to me at the White House."

"That's great—anything else?"

"No more natural disasters!"

I said, "I'm voting for you."

I guess we all have ideas of what life should be like and how we would change things if we could. I tend to know what God should do to make me happier, to change my circumstances, to improve my marriage, to answer my prayers. But even presidents and kings need to submit to the One in charge.

Nebuchadnezzar, the most powerful king of his day, had to learn through humiliation that God was ultimately in control. God told him he would act and live like an animal until he knew that "the Most High rules in the kingdom of men" (Daniel 4:25 NKJV). After what scholars believe was seven years of insanity, Nebuchadnezzar "blessed the Most High and praised and honored Him who lives forever" (Daniel 4:34 NKJV). God sometimes takes drastic measures to remind us to acknowledge Him and not grab glory for ourselves.

I must remember this the next time I try to run my own life instead of submitting to God. And I hope Xander remembers it, too, when he becomes the president.

'Twas the Night Before Grandma's Christmas:
Gratitude

A house needs a grandma in it.
LOUISA MAY ALCOTT

A Bit Like Charlie Brown

ANITA HIGMAN

And if I go and prepare a place for you, I will come back and take you to be with me that you also may be where I am.

JOHN 14:3 NIV

I think God gives grandmothers a special dispensation when it comes to Christmas. My grandmother Metzler was no exception. She loved decorating with lots of glittering tinsel, the more dazzling the better. She would brave the bleakest cold on Christmas Eve just to jingle those reindeer bells outside our windows so we'd know that Santa hadn't forgotten us, and then on Christmas morning she would feed us enough caramelized popcorn balls to keep our dentist busy filling cavities long after the holidays. What's not to love?

To make the holidays even brighter, my grandmother bought a Christmas tree with enough reflective power to rival a solar flare. It was one of those silver metal numbers that looked a bit like the Charlie

Brown tree, only with silver rods for limbs and shredded metallic plumes to represent needles. It had to be *the* most unnatural artificial tree ever created by man. And to make the tree even more flamboyant, Grandma enhanced the spectacle with rotating colored lights. The contraption actually sprayed the tree with alternating primary hues. If people saw that tree today, they would be mortified at its fake and eye-popping gaudiness. But not back then. Not through the eyes of a child. I'm sure I thought it was the most magical and spectacular tree I'd ever seen or ever would see.

It is a universal fact—grandmothers will go to an infinite amount of trouble for their grandkids, and my grandmother was no exception. She resides in heaven now, but I'd love for her to know that even as an adult looking back decades later, I still remember the wonder of it all as she prepared for Christmas. The love-infused moments. The laughter. The feasts. The shimmering decorations. The holy-hushed times of getting to know the true miracle behind Christmas. She held back nothing in preparing for our joy, our awe, and our celebration of Christ!

When I think of where my grandmother is now, in heaven, I think of the scripture reminding us that Jesus went to prepare a place for us—heaven. And right now, He's busy with all the preparations, making all things even more beautiful than our earthly Christmas could ever be.

And I'm blessed to say that there's another universal fact—God will go to an infinite amount of trouble for His children. He will hold nothing back in preparing this heavenly place for our joy, our wonder, and our awe. We will celebrate Christ!

And just imagine, for all eternity, the love-infused hugs, the laughter-filled moments, the feasts that even a grandmother couldn't have imagined or prepared, the magnificent gildings and adornments, and best of all, the joy of getting to know Him—the true miracle behind Christmas.

A Rose or a Radish

ANITA HIGMAN

Jesus asked, "Were not all ten cleansed? Where are the other nine?
Has no one returned to give praise to God except this foreigner?"
Then he said to him, "Rise and go; your faith has made you well."
LUKE 17:17–19 NIV

My grandmother Breitling never had a lot of extra cash for expensive gifts, but she had more than enough generosity to make our presents memorable and magical. On special occasions she would make homemade clothes for my doll. I'm certain those dainty dresses were time-consuming and tedious to cut out and sew, but as I recall, they were well-made and lovely—no sleeves sewn on backward and no crooked lace, just pretty dresses for my doll.

My grandmother also had a flower garden, a rock garden, and a vegetable garden, which came in handy during times of gift-giving. It seemed there was no nook or cranny on her property that she didn't tuck away a rose or a radish or an elephant's-ear plant. I'm surprised she didn't have flowers growing under the rocks. Her thumb was so green she surely came from a family of leprechauns! I inherited some of that love of growing things from watching her in action.

When I was old enough to start my own flower garden, my grandmother gave me a few seedlings, with the roots still attached of course, to put in my garden when I got back home to the farm. She would carefully wrap up the seedlings in a damp towel, and I would then transfer them to my special spots, hoping that my meager plot of land would someday be a paradise. Sometimes my little land of glory was no more than a little patch of mud, but I never stopped hoping and dreaming over that mud!

Eventually those precious doll clothes got put away in the attic, and I'm sure the garden I so carefully tended grew over with weeds long ago. And yet I remember all of it. Even now. . .decades later. I'm sad to say that I can't remember if I ever thanked my grandmother for the dresses sewn with love or the constant flow of seedlings. My heart aches as I write this, wondering if I ever truly appreciated her big-hearted spirit or if I took her kindness and generosity for granted.

As an adult, I've discovered that everyone loves to be thanked—even Jesus. He is constantly looking for ways to give us good things. No shabby gifts but good gifts that make us grin and grow. In the book of Luke we read about Jesus healing a group of ten men. But only one of those men came back to thank Jesus. Only one. And Jesus did notice this lack of praise. I can't help but think how this absence of basic courtesy must have hurt our Lord's heart.

My soul grieves when I recall the times I was given a good gift from the Almighty, even a miracle, and I became one of the nine who didn't return, who didn't bother to come back to praise God.

Lord, I pray that I no longer put Your blessings away in the attic of my heart, but instead run into Your arms with a grateful hug and with praise on my lips!

Grandma's Favorite Things

TINA KRAUSE

Children in whom was no blemish, but well-favored. . .
DANIEL 1:4 KJV

Sometimes I feel like Maria von Trapp from *The Sound of Music*, only better. I "Climb Ev'ry Mountain" and forge every sea through a plethora of toys and games when my grandkids visit. I am *sixty* going on seventeen as I experiment with lip gloss and blush with my almost-thirteen-year-old granddaughter, Mahalet. And I hum the tune to "My Favorite Things" with kid-worthy words: "Cute smiles and laughter and finger-painted pictures, big hugs and kisses and chocolate chip mixtures; granddaughters twirl dressed in pink fairy wings—these are a few of my favorite things!"

Yep, Julie Andrews, spinning on a mountaintop with identically dressed children surrounding her, has nothing on me. After all, I even know who Justin Bieber is!

I do everything for and with my grandkids except handcraft dirndl dresses from window curtains. You want to trek on bikes to the park? No problem. Need another chocolate chip cookie? My pleasure. More orange soda? Sure. How about invading the store for that new toy you wanted? Fun!

Rules are for parents; fun is for grandparents. When I raised my two boys, I used the word "no" more often than signs hanging in public bathrooms. Now *yes* is best. I've learned to reserve negative responses only for those things or elements that would cause my grandchild harm. Everything else is a hearty go.

So when did I get so kid crazy? When did mature, serious parent-hood slip into the enjoyable abyss of childlike reckless abandon? After I realized that being a grandmother is a deserved promotion without all the work.

Being a grandma gives me the opportunity to revisit my childhood through my grandchildren. Six-year-old Kaitlyn and I whisk away to the play area at the children's museum and dawdle for hours. I joke and play games with my teenage grandson Ian and get squirrely with my tween granddaughter Mahalet. I tickle ten-year-old Isaac mercilessly, and I simulate the voices of Buzz Lightyear for four-year-old Alex, or Cinderella for Kaitlyn as I enter my grandchildren's world of make-believe on a moment's notice.

Interestingly, the Lord, too, meets each one of us at our own level of maturity (or, *ahem*. . .immaturity). He wouldn't expect a new Christian to experience the same level of spiritual growth as one who has known the Lord for all of his or her life. Rather, He accepts us where we are and meets us at our level of need.

Grandmas know how to do that with their grandchildren, too.

Maybe that's because grandchildren are our favorite people to enjoy, cherish, nurture, and love. Julie Andrews sang, "The hills are alive with the sound of music." Ah yes, there's nothing better than the symphony of grandchildren. . .except maybe the sound of silence after they leave.

The Wise Man

TINA KRAUSE

Jesus said, "I praise you, Father. . .because you have hidden these things [of God] from the wise and learned, and revealed them to little children."
MATTHEW 11:25 NIV

Years ago, I gave my then two-year-old grandson a cartoon video of the Christmas story during the holidays. As we watched it together, I identified the Bible characters, describing who they were and what they did.

"Who's that?" Ian asked, pointing to King Herod. "That's the bad king," I said with intensity.

Days later, Ian's dad scolded him about something. With furrowed brow, Ian looked up at Jeff and exclaimed, "Daddy, you the bad king!"

Attempting to conceal a smile, Jeff played along. "Ian, if I'm the bad king then who are you?"

Pointing his finger inward, Ian replied, "I the wise man."

One of the greatest holiday joys is celebrating Christmas with my five grandchildren. Just when the holidays become more hassle than happy, one of my blessings will do or say something to lure me away from the land of Scrooge.

On that particular Christmas twelve years ago, I glowed in the reflection of my first grandchild—the little wise man—as he and I celebrated the season, laden with sparkling ornaments and twinkling lights.

Upon my instruction, Ian gingerly cradled the ceramic baby Jesus from my nativity set in his tiny hands, closely examining the figure. We read Christmas-themed storybooks and cruised the neighborhood to admire lighted houses and snow-covered Santas.

God reveals Himself to children, and in order to know God, we must become childlike. Accordingly, how appropriate that Jesus came to earth as a baby. Children symbolize everything that is pure and good. Their innocence and simplicity give us hope, and their smiles and cute gestures soften any hard edges.

God, in His wisdom, presented us with the best gift of all—a babe wrapped in swaddling clothes born in a manger. In Christ, our child-like faith brings promise as layers of sin vanish under the blanket of God's forgiveness and love.

At the end of my grandson's Christmas video, the narrator said that the wise men and shepherds bowed to worship the newborn king.

"Baby Jesus is a good king," Ian observed.

"Yes, Ian," I assured him, "Jesus is a very, very good king who brings us peace and joy at Christmas and always." But then, I suspect he already knew that. After all, Ian is a *wise* man.

Delusions of Grandma:
Relationship

No cowboy was ever faster on the draw than a grandparent pulling a baby picture out of a wallet.

UNKNOWN

What a Giddy Feeling

ANITA HIGMAN

Rejoice always, pray continually, give thanks in all circumstances;
for this is God's will for you in Christ Jesus.
1 THESSALONIANS 5:16–19 NIV

When I was a kid, there were never enough hours in the day to play board games or dominoes or whatever my grandmother Metzler dreamed up for us to play. I think one of my favorite games was Chinese checkers. What fun to race and chase each other around that colorful metal board, trying to get all our marbles lined up. What a great noise that glass ball made as it snapped and popped its way around the board, and what a giddy feeling when it finally made it safely home! I must have squealed with delight. I can almost feel the excitement building as I type this.

And yet, looking back on those rosy days of my youth, maybe it was just as much about Grandma as it was about all the games. I enjoyed spending time with her, and she had lavish amounts of it to spend on me. She was never too busy dusting knickknacks or attending meetings or gallivanting around town. She had serious time on her hands. In fact, if her time were a stream, then it flowed into an ocean—just for me.

I've discovered that God has even more time on His hands than my grandmother did, and He, too, enjoys spending lavish amounts of it on me. I wish I could say that I've always been available for Him as my grandmother was for me, but in all honesty, I haven't been.

Unfortunately, too many times I've rushed through my morning devotions, so quickly in fact that I'm surprised I even bothered to sit down. In Thessalonians I find that I am to pray continually, but I also know that my prayers weren't meant to digress into an hourly Frisbee toss of all my requests.

I think real prayer must be like different notes on a music sheet, that when played together, make a lovely melody—a holy song of praise. Perhaps I need to slow my morning devotions down and ask myself these simple but powerful questions: Have I asked God to forgive me for my transgressions? Have I gone away to a quiet place to listen to His still, small voice? Have I come before Him with a heart of thanksgiving—praising Him for His answers to prayers, His miracles? Have I come before Him in a spirit of awe, expecting fellowship? Have I made my requests known to God?

This full melody of prayer will take more time, more commitment on my part, but I know it will surely make a difference in my daily life. Time was a gift from my grandmother, and it meant the world to me. Surely I can give that same gift back to the One who created me. Give back to the One who wants precious fellowship with me—and with you.

Grandma's Favorite Phone Call

KATHY DOUGLAS

Then they called on the name of Baal from morning till noon. "Baal, answer us!" they shouted. But there was no response; no one answered.

1 KINGS 18:26 NIV

Telephone calls we receive about our grandchildren weave a tapestry of unforgettable beauty. . .sometimes. Sometimes beauty has nothing to do with it. We might hear about our grandson tattooing himself with a permanent marker or our granddaughter making a mess we can easily visualize (but have the good fortune not to experience or clean up). From the time of her first pregnancy, my husband and I received a litany of memorable calls from our daughter Kara.

We well remember the call telling us that Kara, who had been unable to conceive for years, was expecting triplets. Then of course, came the call telling us the boys had arrived. When Kara conceived again—after doctors told her she would probably never have another child—she called to tell us grandson number four would arrive just before his big brothers turned two.

With all the roller-coaster ups and downs of premature triplets and then another little guy, we never lacked for "you need to pray" or "wait till you hear this" accounts via telephone. The phone call that stands out above all the others, however, we saved on our answering machine.

Two days after we had returned from a fun, long-distance visit to our triplet grandsons and their new baby brother, we came home one evening to find a bold, flashing 1 on our phone's message window.

"Grandma and Grandpa," Kara's recorded voice said happily, "it's me."

Then. . .

"Adam, don't hit Mommy." No happy voice.

A pause and a little background noise complete with at least one wailing toddler. The recording continued.

"I wanted to call you because all day Christian has been saying, 'Ganma, Ganpa. . .' "

Then, a bit louder, "Don't bite Christian! Adam, what's with you today?" Brief pause.

"I'm sorry to call during a crisis," she went on more quietly, "but there was no crisis when I originally picked up the pho–"

"Don't hit *him either! No!"*

Our daughter clearly struggled to reset her "outside voice" to conversational level.

"Anyway, Christian's been walking around saying, 'Ganma, Ganpa. . .' "

"*Stop* hitting him. . . !"

Minuscule pause minus anything even *remotely* resembling a giggle.

"Yeah, he's saying a lot of words. . . . NO! You don't hit Mommy. . . ! *NO!* I gotta go. . . ."

Click.

I smile every time I recall that one-sided conversation. And I admit to listening to it every so often on our answering machine. As much as it makes me laugh, though, it's not what I would want if I were the one "calling" God, only to find Him unavailable.

No matter how whiney or even praise-filled my "calls" to God may be, He's never out. Never do I find "no response," or that "no one answered," or "please leave a message." Like the psalmist, I can declare, "I call on you, my God, for you will answer me" (Psalm 17:6 NIV). I cherish and laugh at that telephone message from the mother of my grandchildren, but—thankfully—no abrupt *clicks* come from God on high!

Waiting on the Dirt Pile

Shelley R. Lee

A time to tear down and a time to build up.
A time to weep and a time to laugh;
A time to mourn and a time to dance.
Ecclesiastes 3:3–4 nasb

When Wes was about three years old, his family was building their home in the country. Wes would soon have a tree fort for the first time and so much room to play. He was excited! In the meantime, Mommy and Daddy were very busy with power tools, contractor agreements, inspectors, and other such adult matters. Dirt piles scattered the property resembling a micro hurricane fallout, littered with toys, bikes, tools, food wrappers, and scraps of wood. Wes and his three brothers occupied themselves with downhill dirt races, fort and sculpture building (for lack of a better term), mud games, and the like.

Mommy and Daddy were getting weary. Thankfully Grandma and

Grandpa offered some reprieve when they could. They had taken Wes's oldest brother on a trip to Pennsylvania to visit relatives and would be picking Wes up when they brought big brother home.

Wes couldn't wait to stay with Grandma and Grandpa! He had packed his own little red suitcase with toys and mismatched clothes and waited for Grandma and Grandpa in the front yard on a dirt pile. He did not think about the fact that he was covered from head to toe in grime, a mixture of mud, bugs, lunch, and Kool-Aid.

A hosing down was required when they arrived to pick him up, but he didn't mind. He was happy to be on his way to being the center of attention. It would all be a welcome break from sharing food, toys, and attention with three brothers and preoccupied parents in the throes of home building.

Just as expected, he was indeed the star of the show at Grandma and Grandpa's house. They went on ice cream trips and walks. They went to the store and played outside on the lush lawn, a stark contrast to the hard dirt and clay yard Wes had become accustomed to recently at the building site.

The problem with all this one-on-one attention was that it was so foreign to him. No one competed for the best box of cereal at breakfast time. No one fought with him over the prime viewing seat at cartoon time. There was no one to talk to or get in trouble with right before he drifted off to sleep. He simply couldn't take it anymore. After two days he cried inconsolably to go home. He missed his family so badly that he could no longer function as the little prince at Grandma and Grandpa's. It was all good while it lasted, and there would be times like that again, but this time Wes's daddy had to meet Grandpa halfway to home, at the state line, to return him to the familiar blissful chaos of a family of four boys.

Scary Stuff!

Janice Hanna

The LORD is my light and my salvation; whom shall I fear?
The LORD is the defense of my life; whom shall I dread?
Psalm 27:1 NASB

My granddaughter Maddy and I have a lot in common. We both love great movies, especially musicals. She's particularly crazy about animated movies, as most children are, and can watch them over and over and over again. (Ask me how I know.) Not that I really mind. When I get fixated on a great movie, I can watch it multiple times as well.

One of our recent favorites is a movie titled *Enchanted*. In this sometimes-animated, sometimes-real-people musical, the characters dance, sing, and enchant the viewers with a playful, happy story where fairy-tale characters come face to face with reality in New York City.

Most of the story is happy anyway. There's one section of the movie that's a little scary, and not just to kids. I have a tendency to feel a little nervous during that scene, too.

When we reach that part of the movie, Maddy covers her eyes. "Is this the scary part, Nina?" she asks.

I nod. "Mm-hmm."

"Is the mean lady in this part?"

I nod again.

Maddy's eyes fill with fear. "I don't like this part, Nina!"

I respond, "Me, either!" then fast-forward the movie to the next scene, where wrongs are righted, evil is done away with, and the characters meet up with their happily-ever-after moment. Maddy sighs with relief, uncovers her eyes, and is all smiles once again. Seconds later, she has completely forgotten about the invasive scene. Why? Because she's caught up in the resolution to the story—the good stuff.

Oh, if only life had a fast-forward button like our television remote! Then, when scary moments came, we could simply press the button and zip past them, ready to move on with the good stuff. Unfortunately, we can't avoid the tough seasons, no matter how hard we try. As we walk through them, God develops character in us. He shapes and forms us into stronger, more pliable people.

The next time you feel like covering your eyes to avoid a scary situation, think about it as you would a scene in a movie. Those scenes never last forever. They always give way to a more positive, upbeat ending. Your happily-ever-after is coming. Don't let momentary distractions keep you from your destiny.

A Grandmother's Gift

VALORIE QUESENBERRY

Every good gift and every perfect gift is from above.
JAMES 1:17 NKJV

Andy Rooney is credited with saying, "Elephants and grandchildren never forget."

It seems that with my grandpa, I remember more of what he *said*; and with my grandma, I remember more of what she *did*. Maybe it's because grandmas are always doing things, especially for their grandchildren.

I remember that she taught me how to hand-stitch little pieces of scrap fabric into clothing for my dolls. I sat at the kitchen table and stabbed the poor fabric over and over again with the needle, pulling the thread through in awkward seams. She'd help me unsnarl the thread or tie off the end. And I, of course, was delighted with the finished product.

I recall that she let me help in the kitchen when she whipped up the goodies our family always associated with her. My grandma was a firm believer in doing a project right. Why make only two pumpkin pies when you can make eight? And so her counter and table would be groaning under the weight of numerous loaves of banana bread or dozens of sugar cookies. She'd let me stir the batter sometimes. I'd try to keep it going, but as it got stiffer, I'd have to surrender the spoon back to her. With her sleeves rolled up, she'd go at it with a strength that amazed my little mind.

I recollect that she helped me learn how to drive. Once, on the way home from the grocery store, she let me take the wheel of the little red Ford Valiant for more practice time. After turning onto a side road that would wind us up into the back hills of Tennessee, she told me to stop. And stop I did! Jerked is more like it. That little car practically stood on its hood as I came to an abrupt halt! Unfortunately this was disastrous for the groceries, especially the orange juice, which soaked into the carpet. But my grandmother cleaned up the mess with only a mild commentary on my lack of driving expertise. (Though I believe she took the wheel for the remainder of the drive home!)

There are other things I'll never forget—like the twenty dollars she made me fold into the corner of my wallet when I left for college (in case I was ever without money and had an emergency). There were the times she let me play with her treasured keepsakes and cut out paper dolls and wear her shoes. Spending time with her was a natural and normal part of my childhood. And I know she told me many things. I know she prayed for me. But what I'll always remember are the times I spent with her and the way she let me be part of her world. After all, that's one of the greatest gifts a grandmother can bestow. And it's something a granddaughter will always cherish.

The Dandelion's Hair

BETTY OST-EVERLEY

"The grass withers and the flowers fall,
but the word of our God endures forever."
ISAIAH 40:8 NIV

My mother was an avid gardener. It didn't make any difference whether it was her African violets inside the house, her tulips or roses outside, or even her vegetable garden. She loved to grow plants and spent many an hour doing so. They were her special darlings, and she cared for them almost like a child. If an especially beloved plant died, she was heartbroken.

My daughter, at a young age, learned to love beautiful blossoms and gardening, and because of her grandmother's love for gardening, that wasn't surprising. Whenever Rachel visited Grandma, the conversation would eventually turn to the topic of working in the soil. Sometimes my mother would invite young Rachel to help her outside.

Getting dirty was quite all right as long as something constructive like gardening was being accomplished.

However, having weeds sprout up was something my mother didn't like at all. She would spend a lot of time sitting in her yard pulling weeds. She even knew their names—bull thistle, chicory, bindweed—but none were nearly as hated as the dandelion.

Rachel, on the other hand, thought the dandelion was beautiful. With its bright yellow blossoms, she would pick a handful of them from a plentiful supply in the next yard (whose owner was not nearly as weed-conscious as my mother). Bringing them to Grandma as a present, my mother would feign enjoyment since she didn't want to hurt a five-year-old girl's feelings. But I always knew how she *really* felt about them.

One late summer day, Rachel was enjoying the outdoors while my mother gardened. Leaning over in the neighbor's yard, Rachel started collecting dandelion blossoms.

"Look what I picked for you, Grandma!"

"I see," said Grandma, putting her trowel down so she could accept the gift.

The youngster drew one of the flowers from her bouquet, holding one fragile, white-headed flower in her hand, the breeze rippling through its fluffy tufts.

"Why is this one white, Grandma? What happened to it?"

"That's just its white hair, honey. It got old and decrepit, just like your grandma."

Rachel giggled. Grandma then showed her how to blow the white hair from the dandelion. The head disintegrated and flew away with the breeze. Even a gentle breath from a child can launch the dandelions on a far-flung trip.

The dandelion blossom is here only for a season. After its vibrant yellow bloom turns "old and decrepit," it falls or blows away in the wind. God's Word, however, is sharper than any two-edged sword. It is inspired, "God-breathed," and lives forever. His Word is relevant for all time, all seasons, and all people.

When the wind threatens to blow you away, hold fast to God's Word. You'll survive the storm much better than the dandelion's hair!

Traveling with Grandma: *Joy*

*Grandmas don't just say "that's nice"—they reel back
and roll their eyes and throw up their hands and smile.
You get your money's worth out of grandmas.*

UNKNOWN

Goin' Downhill

KATHY DOUGLAS

I recall all you have done, O LORD; I remember your wonderful deeds of long ago. They are constantly in my thoughts.
PSALM 77:11–12 NLT

Either people get crazier as they age, or they get more creative.

Approaching their senior years, Grandma Lucy and Grandpa Larry moved from flat, northern Ohio to northern Kentucky. No far-reaching, flat miles of road exist there, and snow in northeast Kentucky usually melts by dawn's early light.

Grandma Lucy and her husband live quiet lives. Larry, a former police officer, and Lucy, a retired forklift driver, keep busy living out their well-earned retirements. Most of their excitement now comes vicariously through their grown grandchildren.

Usually.

Unless they get cabin fever.

Which they did during Kentucky's snow-that-didn't-melt-by-dawn's-early-light, or even the *next* dawn's early light in the winter of 2011.

When round one of their persistent snow finally melted, the duo was able to get out and visit their favorite second-hand store.

"Look at these," Larry said to Lucy.

Lucy's eyebrows lifted. "What you got in mind?"

When they got home, Lucy phoned her brother in Ohio.

"Whaddaya think would be the best way to attach a chair to some old skis? Me and Larry are gonna ski."

"You're going to do *what*? With *what*?"

"Well, we live on a mountain, we got snow, and what else we gonna do?"

"Sit on a chair—on skis? You're crazy! Listen," he said, going on gently, "go over to the senior center. Have some hot soup. Play some dominoes. Then go back home to bed. You'll be thinking straight in the morning."

Undeterred, Grandma Lucy thought Grandpa Larry's idea sounded like a good one.

Two snowy days later she watched in admiration as Grandpa Larry flew down their mountain seated on his makeshift ski chair—twice!

"That was fun!" he said after two rides down. (It wasn't quite as much fun carrying the ski chair back *up* the hill.)

"If the snow sticks around, I'll try it," Lucy declared, "tomorrow."

Tomorrow came and Grandma Lucy sat down on the former kitchen chair. With a *whoop* and a *whoosh*, down the hill she went! It was fun until the skis hit bare rock. The ski chair came to an abrupt halt. Lucy did not.

"Fortunately," she said when she reported back to her brother, "the snow made for a soft landing."

Ever feel like you're going downhill only to hit a bump and find yourself airborne and wingless? Bad things get worse. You had a little money, now you've got none. You had a chest cold, now you've got pneumonia. In those times, God's Word encourages us. Look back and remember.

When tough times came to his people, Nehemiah told them, "Remember the Lord, who is great and glorious" (Nehemiah 4:14 NLT). Recalling the Lord—who He is and what He's done—helps us hang on when life throws us for a loop.

Grandma Lucy's chair skiing days may not be over.

"We're lookin'," she confided to her brother, "for an old recliner to screw onto the skis. It'll be more comfortable."

How they'll get *that* back up their mountain remains to be seen.

Pure Potential

TINA KRAUSE

*Being confident of this, that he who began a good work in
you will carry it on to completion until the day of Christ Jesus.*
PHILIPPIANS 1:6 NIV

My grandson Isaac is a born contortionist. If I didn't know better, I'd pledge on my grandmother's pierogi that he bounced out at birth.

From the time Isaac took his first steps, his behavior caused chaos in my son's household. At a young age, Isaac squeezed his tiny frame into any and all crevices. He scaled furniture, tables, and gates with the ease of Spiderman and the agility of a mountain goat. He reached for items double his height with a built-in arm extender to grasp items of choice.

He was the ultimate "Survivor," outwitting, outplaying, and outlasting his mom, dad, and older brother's attempts to control and protect him. As a toddler, he outwitted the child-proof doorknob covers, refrigerator safety latch, and wire mesh security gates designed to keep him out of harm's way, or at least corral him for a few minutes while his mom attempted to get something done.

Even Barney the big purple dinosaur failed to fascinate little Isaac. He was too busy to sit still. Instead he'd run into a wall, bounce off, and stand up without a whimper. A solid wall or concrete driveway seldom stopped Isaac. He tumbled, twirled, jumped, and hurled nonstop.

When he was four years old, his favorite program was *Lazy Town*, featuring a goofy guy who whirls, hops, and runs. The program was created to get kids moving. But Isaac needed the lessons of *Lazy Town* like I need lessons on how to eat Oreo cookies.

While Isaac's antics drove his parents crazy, they amused me. His bursts of energy made me laugh as I wondered what he'd do next to annoy his parents and astound his grandparents. I saw Isaac's potential. If channeled in the right direction, Isaac has the natural abilities of a star athlete, locksmith, or trapeze artist! And his flare for ingenuity will serve him well in anything he attempts.

What we deem negative, the Lord sees as potential, too. By nature, the apostle Peter was impulsive and hotheaded, vacillating from one extreme to another. But after his conversion, God channeled his weaknesses into strengths. He emerged as one of the most courageous champions of the Gospel, willing to endure prison and face death for his faith. After Paul's conversion, God used his passion to present the Gospel with a burning zeal, untiring singleness of purpose, patient suffering, and heartfelt courage.

We are all different and unique. In God's eyes, each individual has special abilities and gifts exclusive to their personalities to fit into His divine plan. Hmm, why is that so hard for parents to understand?

Interestingly, five years after Isaac bounced into this world, his little brother Alex darted out at birth with more energy and cunning than his brother. Alex, wide-eyed, curious, and talkative, can find his way through locked doors and scale countertops in seconds, yet quietly squirms his way between his papa and me while we sleep.

I can't wait to see how God will use Isaac and Alex, my dynamic duo. Meanwhile, I know whom to call if I lock myself out of the house!

Stubborn Etta

JEAN FISCHER

You are nothing more than a stubborn cow—so stubborn that I,
the LORD, cannot feed you like lambs in an open pasture.
HOSEA 4:16 CEV

Great-Grandma Etta was an iron-willed old German woman. She
stood six feet tall and, to put it politely, she had a sturdy build.
When something upset Etta, nobody got in her way.

In the summer of 1900, the telephone company arrived to set
wooden poles and string phone lines on Etta's street. She was eager to
get a telephone, but Etta wasn't thrilled when a workman came along
with a posthole digger. He set the blade at a spot parallel to her front
door and took a bite out of the grassy parkway.

Etta stormed out of the house. "*Vat* are you doing? You *cannot*
put a post *der*!"

The workman was tall, like Etta, and just as broad. "Yeah, well, it's goin' there," he said. "We put 'em an equal distance apart."

Etta threw back her shoulders and raised her chin. "Not in *my* front yard."

He leaned on the handle of the digger. "Lady, this isn't *your* front yard. This part here belongs to the city."

"*Den da* city *vil* have to make *udder* plans," Etta said. "Because I do not give you my permission."

The workman shook his head and plunged the blade of the digger into the ground. He might as well have stuck a knife into Etta's heart. Thank goodness a neighbor came just then and calmed her down.

Great-Grandma Etta stood with hands on hips watching the man dig. "You *vil* not put a post in *dat* hole," she warned. "I *vil* not look out my front *vindow* at an ugly old post!"

The workman ignored her, finished digging, and quickly moved on.

All day long, Etta sat by the window waiting for the post truck to arrive. When it finally rolled down Lake Avenue carrying poles and four workmen, Etta bolted out the front door. Then she did the unthinkable. She sat down on top of the posthole. "Over my dead body!" she shouted to the men.

They tried to reason with her, but she wouldn't listen. They tried to pick her up and get her off the hole, but Etta dug in her heels. Finally someone called the police.

Officer Mahoney walked the beat on Lake Avenue, and he'd spent many summer evenings sipping lemonade on Etta's front porch. "Etta! Why are you sitting there on the ground?" He reached for her hand, and she took it. Believe me, no one else could have gotten Etta off the hole. You see, she trusted Mahoney to do what was right. After only a few gentle words, he convinced Etta to let the men set the post.

Trust means letting go and allowing God to lead you. Are you stubborn like Etta? Are you resisting God? Then reach out and trust Him. Take His hand and let Him pull you off your posthole.

Where Are All the Goldfish?

Jean Fischer

A word fitly spoken is like apples of gold in a setting of silver.
Proverbs 25:11 esv

Nothing compares to autumn in Wisconsin: woodlands blazing with fiery hues of russet and sunset, squirrels hunting for acorns among the pine needles, and brittle oak leaves and warblers singing high in the treetops as they prepare to migrate south.

For Grandma, autumn meant a season of hard work sterilizing mason jars and canning jams, jellies, tomatoes, and peppers. On cool October mornings, she picked the last of the winter squash from their vines and cleaned out the remnants of her vegetable garden. Wearing thick cotton work gloves and rubber goulashes with fur-lined tops, she hauled out the garden hose, scoured the birdbaths and flowerpots, and stored them away in the shed for winter. On calm-wind days, she raked dry leaves into thick piles, set them on fire, and stood watching over the flames. Heaven help anyone who got in her way. Grandma had stern words if they did.

We knew to steer clear of Grandma during this season of canning, cleaning, raking, and storing. In autumn, her patience grew thin, and her words often stung. Grandma always spoke her mind, and gentle reminders to hold her tongue only led to complaining about all the work that waited and how time stole daylight and winter was coming.

Indian summer arrived on a balmy Sunday morning, a gift from God wrapped in blue sky and sunshine. We planned to take Grandma for a drive after church. We decided to go to Holy Hill, a favorite destination, to see the autumn colors. Grandma, predictably, complained about going but finally agreed when we said that it was a sin to work on the Sabbath.

We made the thirty-mile drive north through acres of woodland to the top of the hill thirteen hundred feet above sea level. At its peak sat a Catholic basilica and a shrine dedicated to the Virgin Mary. We got out of the car, walked around a bit, and Grandma, a loyal Protestant, complained all the while.

Finally we arrived at a pool of holy water known for its healing powers. Several nuns stood there praying while the peacefulness of autumn surrounded us. Secretly we felt blessed that Grandma kept silent.

After a few minutes of quiet contemplation, Grandma walked over to where the nuns stood. She gazed long and hard into the pool and studied it from one end to the other. Then, in a loud voice, and to our horror, Grandma said, "So, sisters, where are all the goldfish?"

Job 13:5 says, "If only you would be altogether silent! For you, that would be wisdom" (NIV). If we're not careful, our tongues can get out of control. Like Grandma, we might speak at the wrong time or speak words that sting. The Bible reminds us in Ecclesiastes 5:2 to think before we speak. Doing so leads to words "fitly spoken," words filled with truth, praise, good judgment, and love.

Shop Often and Carry a Big Black Purse

Valorie Quesenberry

She sees that her trading is profitable.
Proverbs 31:18 NIV

My grandmother had a heavy purse. It was one of those bags with a flap that folds over the top and was made of black leather or maybe vinyl and separated by zippered pouches and various compartments. The flap displayed her initials stitched in light-colored thread—*T* and *G* with a big *B* in the middle for Thelma Gertrude Bender. It was an office, drugstore, snack stand, and bank. It was her base of operation.

And it contained some of the niftiest things—like the little golden photo book with magnetic covers that unfolded many times and a collapsible cup made of plastic. Many are the times she dug in that purse and came up with something to occupy me—a pad of paper and pen for writing or a few pieces of candy for eating (my favorites were the nonpareils she sometimes gave me in church!).

Yes, it was a purse a grandmother could be proud of! But its wealth of contents made it quite heavy, and this was very unfortunate for my grandmother, whose love of shopping rivaled the weight of her purse. She especially loved bargains, and the feeling of triumph that comes with getting something cheaper than the advertised price.

As a child, I remember going on shopping trips with my grandmother, watching her glee as she rummaged in the sale bins and haggled with the clerks for a discount on a damaged item. She just couldn't resist a clearance rack and sometimes bought two so she'd have an extra for a friend or to save in case the first one succumbed to wear and tear.

And where was that heavy handbag while she scoped the store and hailed the blue light specials? Why, my grandfather was babysitting it! He'd be sitting on a bench somewhere in the store, holding onto the strap of her big black purse, resting his legs and protecting the bank!

No one could ever accuse my grandmother of being a speedy shopper. For her, shopping was a deliberate act that should be fully savored. She took her time. Finally, when it seemed like we had been there for hours, she'd be ready to go. At the cashier's stand, she'd pull bills from one of the bank envelopes in her purse and pay. And then it was time to lug the purchases home and review the process, exulting in bargains made and pondering whether to go back and get another one (just in case).

I've inherited my grandmother's love of bargain shopping, though my purse cannot compete with the ones she carried. Sometimes when I've scored an especially sweet bargain, I can almost feel her smile of approval. And if there are stores in heaven, I'm certain my grandfather is watching her purse while she flits from table to table.

Grandma University:
Wisdom

If nothing is going well, call your grandmother.

ITALIAN PROVERB

The Wisdom of Grandchildren

ARDYTHE KOLB

*At that time Jesus said, "I praise you, Father, Lord of heaven and earth,
because you have hidden these things from the wise and learned,
and revealed them to little children."*

MATTHEW 11:25 NIV

Many firsts stand out in my memory: first bike, first traffic ticket, and first child, to name a few. Then a most poignant first—a grandbaby. Even though nothing compares to seeing my own babies, I was prepared for those moments. And I had endured hours of labor, so the joy was overshadowed by exhaustion. My reaction was probably a slurred, "Oh, it's a girl (or boy)," before I fell asleep. The awe came a little later.

But with grandchildren, my emotions took over immediately. Things had changed drastically since our babies were born. No more walking along beside the covered wagon the day after giving birth. (Okay, I'm exaggerating, even though a few of the younger kids probably think I'm that old.)

By the time we became grandparents, visitors didn't have to merely peer through the window of the hospital nursery like spectators at a zoo and scan rows of little plastic beds. *Hmmm. . .which one belongs to us?*

We held our first granddaughter within minutes of her birth and marveled at her perfection. We were awed with the realization that she was ultimately a result of the love of parents and grandparents from generations back.

Three years later we took care of Rebekah when our daughter went to the hospital to have their next baby. Naturally, Rebekah could hardly wait. "When can we go see the baby?"

"As soon as your daddy calls to tell us it's born, honey." Debbie and Ed chose not to know ahead of time whether they were having a boy or a girl, so baby was still "it."

"It's taking a long time!"

I could have explained that her mother surely thought it was taking longer than long, but didn't get into that.

We were all thrilled to go meet Jennifer, the new little sister. Rebekah ran into Debbie's room, excited to see Mommy and baby. She scampered up on the bed and accidentally kicked the newborn in the head. "Oops! Sorry Genfer," she said, kissing the spot she'd bumped.

Jennifer learned early to deal with rough treatment (and survive). Both girls were joy-filled and exuberant, full of adventure.

We've learned how refreshing it is to look at life through a child's eyes. Once when the girls were about six and three, they were going swimming and Debbie let Jennifer invite me. "Grandma, can you come to the pool with us?"

"Oh, I don't think so—I'm just too huge."

There was a long pause. Finally she said, "Grandma, the pool's really big." Obviously my vanity was totally confusing to her. I realized I had a lot to learn.

Each grandchild is a new wonder, and they all teach us something special. If we listen to them, we'll understand more clearly what Jesus meant about revealing His truths to children.

When Our Children Become Parents

Ardythe Kolb

When I was a child, I talked like a child, I thought like a child,
I reasoned like a child. When I became a man,
I put the ways of childhood behind me.

1 Corinthians 13:11 niv

Our oldest son never needed much sleep—until he had a baby who didn't sleep through the night. Kevin and Ruth tried all the tricks—soft music, taking Scott for a ride, rocking him to sleep then gently arranging him in the crib—only to watch those sleepy eyes pop open.

When Kevin told us about it, we realized he was getting an unplanned glimpse of what he had put us through. We savored the moment and reminded him of our own sleepless nights.

"What did you do?" he asked.

"It just takes awhile. Children get over it eventually."

"How long is *eventually*?"

"Well, let's see, you're twenty-six. If Scott takes after you, it won't be until he has his own baby. But usually it's just a few weeks."

"How did you survive with five of us?"

"Bunches of love! And you were the only one who didn't need much sleep. When you were two or three you'd patter into our room in the middle of the night and whisper, 'I'm not sleepy. Can we play?'"

Scott didn't keep his parents awake for long, just enough to cause Kevin some concern.

When Scott turned two, there were new challenges. At his birthday party, with no warning, he tossed a Nerf ball and hit my mom, his great-grandma, on the forehead. It didn't hurt, just took her by surprise. With an ornery grin, he said, "You missed!"

About that time he started to test his boundaries. A little boy in daycare frequently said, "Shut up!" Kevin and Ruth stopped Scott when he repeated it. "That doesn't sound nice. We don't say that at our house."

He'd pull his shirt up over his mouth or bury his face in a pillow and whisper, "Shut up. Shut up."

They decided not to turn it into a battle. It didn't take long for him to decide it's no fun if you don't get any reaction.

Kevin was always a picky eater but wanted Scott to try whatever they cooked. One of Kevin's least favorites was oatmeal, but for some reason he thought Scott should make up his own mind about it. So they fixed him a bowl of oatmeal with sugar and cinnamon. He shoved it away, with a scowl on his face.

"Just try one bite. If you don't like it, you don't have to eat it." Scott locked his lips shut.

"Come on," Kevin said, "it won't kill you."

Scott took a tiny bite. Then he immediately fell to the floor—"dead" from oatmeal. It's really hard to remain stern in some situations.

Scott is now in college, a fervent Christian, and still sometimes a clown. As a child, he let people know he had a strong will, and now that strength is a positive influence on others.

Instructing Grandma

Ardythe Kolb

Don't let anyone think less of you because you are young.
Be an example to all believers in what you say, in the way you live,
in your love, your faith, and your purity.

1 Timothy 4:12 nlt

Three of our granddaughters wanted to play hide-and-seek at our house. The youngest was still learning some of the finer points of the game, but she managed to conceal herself in my laundry hamper. I never figured out how she got in without tipping it over.

Once she was in place she couldn't contain the giggles. I was "it" and followed her laughter. "Where's Anna?"

She popped up with a big grin and shouted, "I'm right here, Grandma!"

We laughed as I lifted her out, but then she got serious and said, "You shouldn't put wet things in there. You made me get my clothes wet."

"Sorry. I'll be more careful about that."

We found the other girls and the game continued, but a loud, shattering crash from the bathroom sent me dashing toward the noise. My heart hammered. I imagined a wall mirror that might have somehow fallen, and I had a horrible image in my mind of an injured child.

I found Anna standing in the bathtub. No blood. No broken mirror. Just a wire basket of seashells that used to sit on the rim of the tub for decoration, now scattered in the tub. Relief flooded over me.

But Anna was disgusted—the noise gave away her hiding place. "Grandma! That space is too little for that basket!"

I covered my grin. "I won't put it there again." I didn't mention that the bathtub wasn't designed for hide-and-seek or that pulling a towel off the rack to cover her head had caused the mishap.

Anna looked at me as though I were dense and said, "Let's play something else."

"Good idea. What shall we play?"

"School. I'll be the teacher."

Somehow I figured I'd be the dunce but I'm always ready to make a fool of myself for my grandkids.

Rachael, the oldest of the three, said, "I'd rather read." That's her favorite pastime. "Listen to this chapter, Grandma—it's really foreboding." *Foreboding?*

School was down to two students, but Heather, the other sister, decided to misbehave. She scribbled on her papers, spilled a box of markers, and wouldn't cooperate. Anna's attention turned to controlling her class, but she was unsuccessful. She probably figured both of us were hopeless, so she resorted to a totally unprofessional tactic. She crumpled to the floor in tears. Of course, Heather thought it was funny, but Grandma scooped both girls up in a big hug and tried to smooth the situation.

Anna did an immediate turnaround. "You can't do that. I'm the teacher!" She wiggled out of my arms. Class was back in session and we moved on to coloring.

Playing with grandchildren can teach us wonderful lessons. Kids help us figure out what really matters in life, and how to get over trivial irritations.

Bye-Bye, Nana?

TINA KRAUSE

"Apart from me you can do a nothing."
JOHN 15:5 NIV

Little feet pitter-pattered toward my office as a tiny voice echoed, "Puter! Puter!" I—occupied in another room—yelled, "Ian! Don't go in there!" Too late. By the time I scrambled for my then-two-year-old grandson, he had already booted up my computer.

When Ian turned eighteen months old, I introduced him to a computer program designed for toddlers. Within six months he had mastered level one, but this was the first time he'd sat in Nana's office chair without Nana.

Patiently gazing up at the screen (a real toddler feat), he waited for the icons to appear. Standing alongside him I instructed, "Pumpkin, let Nana click on the program. And don't touch the keyboard yet."

With his chubby hand cupped over the mouse, he glared up at me with his saucer-round brown eyes like a tiny prince seated on an over-sized throne. "No-no-no-no-no-no-no!" he chided. "Bye-bye, Nana."

Bye-bye, Nana? Alas, my two-year-old treasure had created his own language for "Bug off, old girl, I can do this myself!"

I wasn't quite ready for his burst of self-sufficiency. After all, this was the infant I'd cradled to sleep, assisted in first steps, taught to build blocks, identify shapes, and recite ABCs. And already he's communicated his desire for independence?

Perhaps God feels the same way about us. Have you ever felt inadequate to complete a project or overwhelmed with unfinished tasks? Frustrated and fatigued, you sought God for assistance until relief came. Conversely, when your confidence swells and you feel secure, how much time do you spend in prayer? Do you balk when respected family members or friends offer suggestions? Do you reject God's direction, insisting you can manage on your own?

In everything God desires our faith to remain childlike, but not our behavior. Our dependence on Him produces the spiritual maturity we need to adjust poor attitudes, build strong relationships, handle tough problems, and accomplish difficult tasks. Godly dependence grounds us spiritually and keeps us teachable so that we, in turn, can help others.

As for my technological tiny tot? Moments after he erratically clicked the mouse and pounded on the keys, the program went berserk and I had to intervene. But all too soon, he mastered the computer on his own and now he instructs me.

But bye-bye, Nana?

No-no-no-no-no-no-no.

Our Little Prophet

TINA KRAUSE

Out of the mouth of babes and sucklings hast thou ordained strength.
PSALM 8:2 KJV

When he was four years old, our grandson Ian loved to imitate Bible characters, having memorized entire Bible videos. Teasingly, I called him our "little prophet boy."

So when we vacationed in Tucson, Arizona, young Ian was in his element. He had all the landscape and props necessary to perform his Bible stories. While in Sabino Canyon Desert, Ian neared a tumbleweed—aka Moses' burning bush—and picked up a stick on the roadside. With more drama than Charlton Heston, he approached the prickly plant, thrust his makeshift staff to the ground, pretended to remove his sandals, and knelt beside the bush to talk to God. My husband and I looked on, careful not to interrupt his play, as our little prophet acted out his scene. "He's playing Moses," I offered to onlookers as they strolled past, smiling.

Another day, the outdoor cave at Sonora Desert Museum served as a backdrop for scenes from his video *Jonah and the Whale.*

"*Jo-nah! Jo-nah!*" Ian bellowed in his authoritarian God-voice. Quickly, he switched characters: "What is it, Lord?"

God: "*Go to Nineveh. I have a job for you to do.*"

Jonah: "But I don't want to go to Nineveh; the Ninevites are wicked people."

God: "*Jonah, I want you to tell the Ninevites of My love. For I love the Ninevites, as I love the Israelites, as I love ALL people.*"

In sync with the story line, Ian fast-forwarded to the tossed-overboard-and-swallowed-by-a-whale segment. He (Jonah) mimicked the whale spitting him onto dry ground. Lying on his side with one arm stretched above his head, Ian issued stage instructions to me.

"Nana," he directed me, "you be the Ninevites." As I positioned myself, Ian stood up, stretched out his arms, and exclaimed, "People of Nineveh, turn from your wicked ways!"

Ian recited Bible stories like most preschoolers memorize nursery rhymes. Before our holiday dinner he narrated the entire Christmas story. What's more, he knew more Bible trivia than anyone else in the family (I can't name all of Joseph's brothers!).

As I observed Ian's simple faith, heartfelt innocence, and desire to learn, I saw God at work. It's incredible how the Lord manifests His love and leading in small children.

When Ian's parents were expecting another baby, they prayed about a name for their new addition. But no matter what name they suggested, Ian insisted otherwise. "The baby's name is Isaac," he'd state with conviction.

"How cute," everyone said. But when Ian announced his brother's name to me it sounded right. "After all," I reminded his parents, "how can you refute Moses? Just look what happened to Pharaoh when he did!"

Parents and grandparents focus on the lessons we must teach our children, but God sometimes reveals the lessons that children can teach us.

The prophet Isaiah said, "And a little child shall lead them" (Isaiah 11:6 KJV). Hmm, I wonder if he had Ian in mind at the time?

Back on Track

LINDA HOLLOWAY

*Let us run. . .the appointed course of the race that is set before us,
looking away [from all that will distract] to Jesus.*
HEBREWS 12:1–2 AMP

*C*lick. *Click.*

I shifted in my chair, trying to ignore the ballpoint pen's sound. The lesson plan indicated spelling for that time slot, and the book lay open on the dining room table. My thirteen-year-old grandson sat across from me, silhouetted in the morning light. Again and again he clicked the pen. *Maybe soon he'll start to work without a reminder.*

Click. Click.

I sighed. "Will you write the spelling words or use them in sentences first?"

Click. Click.

My attempt to redirect his attention had failed.

Hands clenched, I took a deep breath. *Homeschooling one kid can be as trying as teaching a roomful.* Like a leaky faucet the repetitive clicks grated on my nerves. Finally, I tapped the table. "*Shiny?*" I said.

Click. "Huh? What?"

"I said, *shiny.*"

He frowned. Then his eyebrows flew up. "Oh, yeah, *shiny.*" He wrinkled his forehead. "What was I suppose to be doing?"

"Spelling."

He nodded, clicked the pen once more, and wrote a few words. After his noisy side trip, he returned to the day's lesson.

While he worked, I thought about *shiny.* I recalled a cheerful barista at the coffee shop. One morning she had disappeared from the counter mid-conversation. I glanced down to pick up my hot cappuccino as I completed my side of our chat. Soon I discovered that I apparently was talking to myself.

Suddenly she popped up from behind the bakery case. "I'm so sorry. I have ADHD (attention deficit hyperactive disorder)." She pointed at an imaginary object. "It's like 'O-o-o, shiny.' And *bam!* I'm distracted."

I told her story to my grandson, who also has ADHD. We used the word *shiny* as a reminder to ignore the distraction. . .get back on track. . .focus.

In fact, he's also said the code word to me. One spring afternoon we broke from studies to walk and talk in the fresh air. (Actually, he did most of the talking.) When a flash of red zipped overhead, I stopped. Then I stepped closer to the tall oak. Craning my neck, I attempted to spot the cardinal among the leaves.

"Grandma?"

I turned my head and lowered my gaze to his. His mischievous grin puzzled me. "What's the matter?" I asked.

"*Shiny*, Grandma."

I chuckled, nodded, and rejoined him on the sidewalk.

In our daily lives it's possible to experience spiritual ADHD. Shiny distractions lure us, from annoying neighbors to terrorist threats, social media to "reality" TV shows, or runaway thoughts to runaway pride. We can choose either to keep our eyes on Jesus or to wander off. The good news is, we don't have to run our specially designed course alone. As I cued my grandson to get back on track, the Holy Spirit cues us. Will we resume the race?

Need Help?

Shelley R. Lee

*"Who is the greatest in the kingdom of heaven?" And calling
to him a child, he put him in the midst of them and said,
"Truly, I say to you, unless you turn and become like children,
you will never enter the kingdom of heaven."*

MATTHEW 18:1–3 ESV

When he was about four, Trevor was staying overnight at Grandma and Grandpa's house. Trevor loved to draw, create, and work on art projects. He asked Grandma if she wanted to join him in drawing. Grandma was totally game for this project. It was reminiscent of her own father sitting down to draw with her daughter, Trevor's mother. This was a sweet opportunity that she would not miss.

They set up their drawing paper and an assortment of pencils and crayons on the table.

"Let's draw boats in water," Trevor said.

Grandma thought she could handle drawing a boat; it was going to be nice, actually. All set in their seats, they began the drawing process, each concentrating on their individual work.

What Grandma didn't know was how frequently Trevor sat and drew. She also didn't know how frequently he drew boats in the water. He had a certain type of scene that he liked and had become very good at drawing. It began with the shape of the big sailboat and a few waves. Then behind the sail he drew in layers of mountains on what looked to be an island. Then he would fill in the sky and water detail, and lastly add color.

How a four-year-old could draw something like this was beyond Grandma. It seemed that he had watched the soothing-voice painter guy on PBS a few too many times. Regardless, he knew how to nail this scene.

Trevor was finished first, so while waiting for Grandma he did a little more shading and touching up. When Grandma announced she was finished, Trevor took a look at her boat in water and paused. He looked at Grandma, then back at the drawing with a tilted head, and then uttered, "Maybe my dad can help you."

Grandma just laughed and laughed at that, but the truth was, her young grandson's picture was much better. She could probably learn a lot more about drawing boats by watching this four-year-old.

It's kind of funny how we think we are always the ones to teach the children. Then we learn from them, too.

Another time, Trevor's brother wiggled out of his socks by sliding his feet backward on the carpeting. Grandpa asked what he was doing. "This is how I take off my socks," he said with a big smile.

Later Grandma saw that become a habit for Grandpa. "I learned something! It's much better this way," Grandpa said.

We are instructed to be like children. But which of the great things about children is Jesus referring to? Innocence? Faith? Having fresh eyes and minds for learning? Perhaps we should just aim to be all of the above.

Ancient Wisdom

CONOVER SWOFFORD

With the ancient is wisdom; and in length of days understanding.
JOB 12:12 KJV

Ann's two grandchildren, Charlie and Amy, were visiting her for the week. By Tuesday they were bored with everything at her house. Ann decided to take them to see the infantry museum at nearby Fort Benning, Georgia. Both children were impressed with all the exhibits at the museum. Ann decided to impress them further. "Before this building was used for the museum, it was the hospital here," she told them, "and I was born in that hospital." Charlie looked at her and said with awe, "Granny, I knew you were old. . .but I didn't know your were a museum piece!"

Our children, and especially our grandchildren, have a tendency to think that we are old; so old that we've forgotten what it's like to be young. They think that we're cramping their style or just being mean or giving them grief when we restrict their activities. Maybe we think that way about God sometimes. We forget how much He loves us and that everything He's doing is what's best for us. We want what we want.

There is a Pennsylvania Dutch saying: We grow too soon old and too late smart. The Bible says we are to be as wise as serpents and as harmless as doves. But we are not to be wise in our own eyes. The Bible warns us time and again about not getting ourselves puffed up about what we know. We can't let our understanding go to our heads. We are to obtain and maintain a heart of wisdom.

The book of Proverbs is full of good advice on how to do this. Basically it says that we must seek after wisdom. Wisdom isn't just learning and it isn't just knowledge. It doesn't automatically come with age. But as we get older we should get wiser. We should be able to apply the learning and knowledge we have acquired. James 1:5 gives us the simple answer—if we lack wisdom, God will give it to us if we ask. Then we need to share that wisdom with our children. Deuteronomy 6:7–9 says that we are to be so committed to teaching our children (and our grandchildren) the commandments of the Lord at every opportunity, that we will tell them about God when we're sitting, walking, lying down, and rising up. It says that we are to write them on the doorposts of our houses. We can decorate our walls with Bible verses on plaques. We can write verses on 3x5 cards and put them where we will see them. Our grandchildren will see them when they come to visit. Then we can explain the meaning of the verses. We can also teach them to memorize the verses. The Ancient of Days has all the wisdom we will ever need, and He wants us to share it with our grandchildren.

The Daredevil Spirit

JANICE HANNA

For God has not given us a spirit of fear and timidity,
but of power, love, and self-discipline.
2 TIMOTHY 1:7 NLT

Of my six grandchildren, only two are daredevils. They happen to be siblings. Ethan, two, is afraid of nothing. Maddy, four, will try everything at least once. Can you even imagine how scary it is to watch the two of them for several hours? The potential for chaos is immense!

About a month ago I went to their house for a visit. While there Maddy asked if she could show me a new trick she'd learned on the trampoline. I watched as she did a perfect flip. My applause came naturally, of course. Enjoying my accolades, she decided to do the trick again. This time, however, she wasn't as cautious. She was far too interested in watching my reaction to pay attention to her movements and she lost her focus. Landing on the top of her head, she cried out in pain.

For a moment I was genuinely worried that she'd done serious damage to her neck. Praise the Lord, that turned out not to be the case. She was more shaken than anything.

Once she calmed down, I felt sure Maddy would come inside the house, leaving the trampoline for another day. No chance. Within minutes she was back outside, jumping up and down and eventually flipping, flipping, flipping, as always. In other words, fear hadn't stopped her from doing what she loved. She forged ahead, more determined than ever.

Perhaps Maddy's daredevil spirit was a little dangerous, but at least she didn't let fear lock her in its grip. How many times do we do that? We want to take a step of faith, but we're paralyzed by fear—especially when life has already injured us in some way. We're too scared to get back on the trampoline and try again.

The Bible tells us that God hasn't given us a spirit of fear (or timidity). Rather, He's given us the internal fortitude—courage—to face the scary things head-on. Sure, there will be plenty of bumps and bruises along the way, but we can't let those stop us. They're not permanent injuries.

Today, if you're feeling afraid, don't let fear hold you in its grip. Look fear in the face. . .then take a giant step forward. Allow the Lord to embolden you with His courage so that you can live life as a spiritual daredevil, ready to face any challenge.

The Fruit of Her Hands

VALORIE QUESENBERRY

*Give her of the fruit of her hands, and let
her own works praise her in the gates.*
PROVERBS 31:31 NKJV

My mother's mother could probably outdo the Proverbs 31 lady in some aspects. She's a fantastic cook (pies are her specialty), a gardening genius, a gifted seamstress, and a frugal homemaker.

My earliest recollections of my maternal grandmother center on the food that she'd grown and canned or frozen. For years I associated her with homegrown sweet corn. There is nothing better on God's earth than Indiana sweet corn cut off the cob and simmered with butter, salt, and pepper. I can imagine the taste and texture even now.

The other item from her garden that I vividly recall is strawberries. They were delightful to eat right from the plant or in her home-made jam.

My grandma's kitchen has homey wallpaper, an upright freezer, and a countertop stove. It isn't lavish or large. In fact, its size is very misleading. She has created fabulous meals in that small space. To be a good cook, you don't need an industrial-size kitchen or a gigantic garden. Growing food and cooking it just requires passion and the willingness to try.

My grandma had both, but even she had to improve her skills over the years. Her first attempts at real cooking were at an early age. At fourteen she became a live-in nanny, keeping house and tending children—first for friends and then for an older sister. During this time, she fixed her first batch of fried chicken. After breading the pieces and placing them in hot oil, she took them out sizzling and golden brown. But the first bite revealed an unpleasant surprise: only the outside was crispy brown; inside, the meat was nearly raw.

And she had a few strike-outs in housekeeping as well. Bleach was the newest cleaner for homemakers in that day, and my grandma decided to try it on her sister's washcloths. On wash day, she poured some on each cloth, right in the center where they were usually stained. Then she hung them up on the clothesline. She testified that they were spotless and shining white. But, alas, she didn't know to rinse out the bleach, and the fabric fibers disintegrated. When her sister picked up a cloth to wash with, her hand went right though it!

Even her sewing skills had humble beginnings. She recalled that my grandfather teased her about the first outfits she sewed for her little daughter, my mother.

But she persevered and became a fabulous cook, thrifty housekeeper, wonderful seamstress, and gardener extraordinaire. It's difficult for me to imagine my grandma not doing well in these areas. In my mind, they always defined her. But, just as baby seeds need time to become lush plants, so the fruit of a woman's hands ripens through the years. And, in my grandma's case, her legacy is a veritable orchard; it has greatly sweetened my life.

Spare Parts

BETTY OST-EVERLEY

You should clothe yourselves instead with the beauty
that comes from within, the unfading beauty of a
gentle and quiet spirit, which is so precious to God.
1 PETER 3:4 NLT

When my brother and his family made the long road trip from Texas to Missouri to visit my mom, she made room in her small house to accommodate them. She would often offer her room to my brother and his wife and gave the other bedroom to the two grandchildren. Mom would take the sofa bed in the front room and use the coffee table as her dressing table, where she placed her personal items.

Because they lived so far away, the grandchildren really didn't get to see their grandmother very often—usually only twice a year. There were lots of knickknacks in her house that were curiosities to young children, and for the most part, Mom was very forgiving about their explorations.

One morning, Mom got up before everyone else and started preparing breakfast. Wonderful smells wafted upstairs, awakening the rest of the family. As they bounded downstairs, four-year-old Mark saw Grandma on the sofa bed, putting a battery into her hearing aid. The device piqued his curiosity, and he started to reach for the second hearing aid.

"No, no, Mark, you can't touch that," my mom gently said to her grandson. "Those are really expensive and I'm sorry, but you can't play with them."

He gave her a hurtful look. It seemed so out of character for Grandma to tell Mark "no" about his curiosity.

"Those are Grandma's ears," she said, gently taking the other hearing aid from his small hands.

"That's funny, Grandma. Those aren't ears!"

"Yes they are, honey. These are Grandma's ears." Pointing to a container on the coffee table, she said, "In that cup are Grandma's teeth."

She lifted the lid so he could see a full set of dentures. His eyes got large.

Mom then picked up her eyeglasses. "And these are Grandma's eyes."

Mark giggled loudly. Mark wore glasses and seemed to understand that one.

"And this," picking up her cane beside her, "is Grandma's wooden leg!"

Mark's giggles turned into uproarious laughter.

"So you think that's funny? Just wait until you have a bunch of spare parts, just like Grandma!"

Some people spend lavishly on fashionable clothing or emulate famous movie stars' hairstyles. None of that really interests God. He is looking for the beauty of a kind, gentle spirit. Mom could have reacted sharply to a young child wanting to play with expensive medical equipment. Instead, she used humor and gentleness in this very teachable moment. Her attitude was firm, yet loving.

Mom isn't concerned about all her "spare parts" because she knows drawing close to the Lord will clothe her better, in the form of a quiet and gentle spirit. What adornments are you investing in?

To Grandma with Love:
Compassion

A garden of love grows in a grandmother's heart.

UNKNOWN

Generations' Transformations

ARDYTHE KOLB

For the LORD is good and his love endures forever;
his faithfulness continues through all generations.
PSALM 100:5 NIV

I love to watch children. Newborns are irresistible to me. Toddlers make everybody chuckle. School-age kids are still at that wonderful "wow!" of discovery. Teenagers. . .well, not so much. But then they get married and start their own families, and the cycle is renewed, with interesting changes.

Every generation is unique, and each one seems to accumulate more stuff. When our children were little, my mother marveled, "It looks like they have every toy available." By the time we were grandparents, kids had a lot more—an endless assortment of entertainment. Now we have a great-granddaughter, and it boggled my mind to see what was necessary even before she arrived.

Her nursery is a decorator's delight and is equipped with amazing conveniences. Our first daughter occupied a crib-sized corner of our one-bedroom apartment. By the time her brother was born, we lived in a small house, but baby shared a room with his big sister. We added more bedrooms and more children, but room-sharing continued through five kids. We never did have a nursery.

Our granddaughter was astounded when we talked about those days. "The only equipment we had to have was a crib, a high chair, and a diaper pail," I said.

"What's a diaper pail?"

I forgot—she's only known disposables. "We used cloth diapers," I explained. "I rinsed them and tossed them in the pail until it was time to do laundry."

"Ewww! That's disgusting!"

Another change is that today's babies can't leave the hospital without a car-seat that meets government specifications. And there's a vast array of innovative contraptions to make caring for babies safe and easy.

Even giving birth is no longer the same. I made the mistake of telling our expectant granddaughter, "Grandpa would have been flat on the floor if he had to watch the delivery of our babies. Fathers-to-be stayed in a waiting room."

She was horrified. "But Grandma, who coached you through labor?"

"Would you believe that billions of babies were born before anyone dreamed of having coaches?" She was speechless.

I continued to amaze her with tales of the olden days. "Babies were kept in the hospital's nursery and only brought to the mothers a few times a day. No one was allowed to visit, even the fathers, when babies were in our rooms."

"Why?"

"That's just the way it was. They wanted to protect newborns from germs as much as possible."

"Really?"

As soon as our great-granddaughter arrived, family and friends flocked to the hospital to meet, cuddle, and kiss the tiny new person. And countless photos were immediately posted on Facebook.

Change may be good, but some things always stay the same, like the love parents feel for their children. Only our heavenly Father understands deeper love, and He freely offers it to each of us. Every new generation can praise Him for His indescribable love and faithfulness.

My Space? Not Anymore

Tina Krause

"Love the Lord your God with all your heart and with all your soul."
Matthew 22:37 NIrv

Shortly after our first grandchild was born, I emptied one of my dresser drawers to fill with his items. Appropriately, I labeled it Ian's Drawer. This is where new toys and picture books would reside, awaiting curious eyes to see and chubby hands to explore each time he came for a visit.

Twenty months later, Ian's drawer evolved into Ian's house. And fourteen years and four additional grandchildren later, my house has turned into a virtual playground and teenage hangout. Age- and gender-appropriate toys and items from Barbie to Buzz Lightyear bulge from baskets, hampers, and closets. Reminders of my grandchildren are everywhere from tiny smudge prints to adult-size footprints.

Like a kids' clothing store, five different sizes of clothing—from bathing suits to dress shirts—occupy my office closet next to a set of drawers crammed with kids' socks, underwear, and pajamas for when any or all of my grandkids spend the weekend. Sippy cups and character bowls line kitchen shelves for our two smallest treasures.

Yep, the grandkids have invaded my space, disrupting the peace and snatching my time with giant hugs and frequent visits. And I love it.

Actually, my husband and I have never experienced much time as empty nesters. You know, that cycle of life when parents can choose to sleep in or dash out at a moment's notice without having to get a babysitter, pack a diaper bag, or recite a list of *don't-do-this-while-I'm-gone* instructions.

Our grandkids—Ian, Mahalet, Isaac, Kaitlyn, and Alex—occupy our home and hearts, giving us more joy than if we received a truck-load of Oprah's favorite things. And all we have to do is open the front door.

A similar phenomenon occurred when I asked Christ into my life. At first I thought God would reside in only a few areas reserved especially for Him—a space here, a crevice there. But I soon discovered that to love God is to place Him first, surrendering every room of my spiritual house to Him.

Amazingly, I wanted to spend time with Him, and I desired to know more about Him and His will for my life through His Word. Only then could my relationship grow. Jesus desires first place in our space to dispense His forgiveness, grace, and love in every nook and cranny of our lives.

My love for my grandkids compels me to open every part of my home and my heart to their presence. My love for God does the same. Thirty-five years ago, Christ entered each room of my home and every place in my heart. Today, my grandkids run a close second!

Grandmas Get It

Tina Krause

*"Don't let the wise boast in their wisdom or the powerful
boast in their power or the rich boast in their riches
But those who wish to boast should boast in this alone:
that they truly know me, and understand that I am the Lord."*
Jeremiah 9:23–24 nlt

Whenever my twelve-year-old Ethiopian granddaughter and I spend time together, we laugh, joke, tease, and get downright silly. Alone in the house, we sing louder than storm-warning sirens. And, I might add, the cacophonous sound is just as piercing.

She's my BFF. Despite her underdeveloped English vocabulary, we communicate great—verbally, spiritually, and emotionally.

Mahalet is tall, regal, and beautiful. So much so, people often stop and comment on her model-like features. I've often told her she could wear a garbage bag and still grace a magazine cover. But beyond her exterior beauty, she's a sensitive, caring, intuitive, and perceptive girl, discerning far beyond her twelve years. She's spiritually connected and wants to know God more.

"Grandma," Mahalet said one day as we cruised through the neighborhood sipping vanilla shakes, "thank you for understanding me." I turned and hugged her with my eyes. I instinctively know Mahalet. Since she has the gift of gab, I know when something's wrong the minute silence envelops the room. If she pauses to speak, she's not merely searching for words—she's withholding information I might not want (but need to) hear; and if she grins with a glint in her eye, she's about to pull a prank.

Let's face it. A grandma, whether through adoption or birth, has an innate ability to understand her grandchild. For instance: Long before our grandchild utters their first words, a grandmother gets it. If a toddler spits green beans into his milk, he's experimenting with colors. If she blurts out, "No!" she's merely communicating a thought she is unable to fully express. If he scribbles crayons across the table, it is because his precocious gift of artistry outshines an 8x10 piece of paper. If a new toy loses her interest, it is due to our grandchild's exceptional mental capabilities. When he squirms in his car seat announcing, "I'm stuck!" we declare our own seat-belt restrictions, replying, "I'm stuck, too!" And when our grandchild says, "Grandma, you understand me," we know exactly what that means.

God understands us, too. Adopted into the family of God, we enter His kingdom broken and confused. Our outward appearance may reflect a confident, "together" person, but our inner heart speaks otherwise. Without hesitation, the Lord embraces us with love and forgiveness; He meets us where we are, just as we are. What's more, He wants us to know and understand Him, too.

When one of my grandchildren speaks from his or her heart, I intuitively listen from mine. When we speak from our hearts, God listens, too. He is the Supreme Grandparent because He knows us better than anyone and still gets it!

Family Love

LINDA HOLLOWAY

Children are a gift from the LORD; they are a reward from him.
PSALM 127:3 NLT

What a fun celebration! Bret, my stepson, Josh, my step-grandson, and I partied at our favorite ice cream shop. The May sunshine streamed across our table. I closed my eyes and enjoyed the warmth on my back as I waited for my Mother's Day treat. Bret brought my yummy flavor combination, peanut butter fudge and pecans.

"Josh, you didn't wait for us," Bret said and frowned.

Eight-year-old Josh raised his head and grinned. Blue decorated his mouth, teeth, and tongue. Then he resumed vigorously licking his "favoritest" flavor, bubble gum, and pushed a pretty pink and white bag toward me. "Here, Grandma. Open your gift."

First I read my card. Its sweet message blurred before my eyes. Then I lifted my present from its nest of tissue paper. The mosaic cow was a reminder of the Cows on Parade art exhibit Josh and I visited the previous summer.

Josh abruptly changed the conversation in the midst of my oohing and ahhing over my gift. "Grandma, do we have the same blood?"

"What do you mean?"

"Do you have any of the blood me and Dad do?"

"No."

His brown eyes widened. "Not even one drop?"

"Not one."

Josh whipped around and stared at his father. "Then why are we celebrating Mother's Day?"

"Because she's been like a mother to me."

Josh shrugged and resumed his attack on the cone. I smiled and wiped a tear from my cheek.

When God brought Jerry into my life, He also brought three teenage children. At the time I didn't think about being a grandmother. Since the two boys lived with us, being a stepmother loomed large in those years. It was a challenge, and sometimes I could hardly imagine past high school. . .or even the next day. But the years passed in rapid succession. One evening we received the phone call: "You're going to be grandparents."

Me? A grandmother? I wondered how that would work out in our blended family.

I'm honored that God gave me the opportunity to grandparent, even though I never birthed a child. I told Josh from the time he was a little guy, "You always hug Grandma, no matter how old you get." He'd nod with a serious expression, and then we'd both giggle.

Years later, even when Josh appeared to be in teenage angst, he still hugged me in greeting and before parting. "Love you," I'd say.

"Love you," he'd respond.

My heart would melt, and I'd smile, touched by family love.

All children need assurance of love. When God places them in our lives, He offers us an opportunity to bless and to be blessed. He also gives us grace to develop relationships that can make a difference in their lives. In addition, we can experience the reward God calls children. Maybe not instantly. Maybe not for years. But reward will come.

Just Call Me Nina

JANICE HANNA

"Do not fear, for I have redeemed you;
I have called you by name; you are Mine!"
ISAIAH 43:1 NASB

I am the grandmother of six children under the age of five. When my oldest granddaughter, Madysen, was born, my daughter asked the obvious question: "What do you want your grandchildren to call you?" I thought about my answer long and hard. Whatever name I chose would stick with me for years to come, so it needed to be a good one. "Grandma" was the word everyone called my mother. Every time I heard the word, I thought of her. Besides, I didn't feel old enough to be a grandma. I've since learned that a lot of us first-time grandmothers feel the same way!

For days I toyed with ideas: Grams, Grammy, Mee-Maw, Mumsey, Grand Doll. . .you name it, I heard it suggested by my friends who'd all walked this road before me. After a bit of reflection, I settled on "Nana." I loved the name. Felt just right. Never mind the fact that it was the name of the dog in *Peter Pan*. I found it to be the perfect fit, particularly since it rhymed with my maiden name, Hanna. I would be Nana Hanna.

My daughter and son-in-law started calling me "Nana" every time Madysen was around. We felt sure she would catch on. However, about the time she turned a year and a half, she came up with her own name for me: "Nina." I would smile and correct her each time. "No, honey. Not Nina. *Nana*." She would grin, eyes sparkling, and say, "Nina!" then throw her arms around my neck, melting my heart in the process and making the issue seem pretty insignificant. After a while, the label "Nina" just stuck. It felt good to know she'd given me her own special name—far better than choosing a name for myself.

To this day, my grandchildren call me *Nina*. No, it wasn't my name of choice. It was *their* name of choice. Something that felt right to them. And for that, I'm tickled pink.

In the same way Madysen called me by her special name, God calls me by name, as well. He calls me "chosen." He also calls me "set apart." He calls me His child, His beloved, His creation. Sure, I might try to revert to my old names: spoiled, pampered, self-centered—but He gently reminds me that letting Him name me is for the best.

Which name do you go by? Remember, choosing for yourself isn't half as much fun as letting others come up with something on their own. Let those grandbabies (and the Lord) label you. Trust me. . . anything they come up with will make you feel like a million bucks!

Feliz Cupleaños. . .
Happy Mother's Day?

Janice Hanna

The LORD your God is with you, the Mighty Warrior who saves.
He will take great delight in you; in his love he will no
longer rebuke you, but will rejoice over you with singing.
Zephaniah 3:17 NIV

I live near the Gulf Coast, in the state of Texas. Two of my grandbabies live on the opposite side of the country from me in Missoula, Montana. Talk about heartbreaking. The separation is tough! Thank goodness for unlimited minutes on my cell phone, along with social media sites, where we can share photos and videos. Of course we still communicate via e-mails and text message as well. We're able to stay in touch as never before.

Awhile back I got a funny message from my daughter, sharing a story of something my three-year-old granddaughter Avery had done.

It tickled me then and still makes me laugh even now!

Avery wanted to shop for a card for Mother's Day. Her daddy (Brandon, my son-in-law) took her to Wal-Mart and said, "Pick out any card you like for Mommy. Anything at all! The sky's the limit!"

She searched long and hard, looking through dozens—if not hundreds—of cards. Finally she stumbled across the perfect one. Stunned, Brandon said, "Are you sure?" Avery responded with a nod and a delightful smile. The card was purchased and taken home. Once there, Avery took great pains to write her name inside the card and the word MOMMY on the envelope.

Imagine my daughter's surprise when she opened her Mother's Day card from Avery and saw that it was a "Dora" birthday card, written in Spanish. Funnier still, when Courtney opened the card, it began to sing "Feliz Cupleaños" (Happy Birthday) quite loudly, in Spanish of course.

Avery got a big kick out of this. She squealed with delight, knowing she'd purchased the perfect card for her mommy one she'd chosen with great care. Her celebration over her mom's special day was made perfect because of that card. It didn't matter what the card said. It was a direct reflection of her heart for her mother; the ideal offering for the occasion.

In many ways, the story of Courtney's Mother's Day card reminds me of God's great delight over us. Did you know that the Bible says He celebrates over us with singing? It's true! Every time we spend a few moments with Him, it's like opening a birthday card and hearing that triumphant, joyous song ring out all over again.

Our loving heavenly Father delights in giving us perfect gifts that are sure to please. They're hand-picked and not always what we expect—but usually so much more! What an awesome God we serve!

A One-Handed Easter Egg Hunt

JANICE HANNA

But a Samaritan, as he traveled, came where the man was;
and when he saw him, he took pity on him. He went to him and
bandaged his wounds, pouring on oil and wine. Then he put the
man on his own donkey, brought him to an inn and took care of him.
LUKE 10:33–34 NIV

My granddaughter Peyton has always been quite a character. Her adorable curls and engaging smile could melt anyone's heart. That precious pixie can make me laugh no matter what she's facing. Such was the case when she recently sustained an injury to her hand and arm. Peyton was released from the hospital just in time for our family's annual picnic and Easter egg hunt. We were so excited to think that she could actually participate. On the day of the big event, we handed her a lovely Easter basket and sent her off to hunt for eggs alongside the other children.

Unfortunately we forgot that with one hand completely bandaged, she had no way to actually pick up the eggs. Poor little thing! She clutched the basket with her "good" hand and stared down at the eggs. Clearly she couldn't figure out what to do. How could she fill her basket with no free hand?

Instead of crying about it, she looked up at me and shrugged, as if to say, "Oh well." Talk about having a great attitude!

Just about the time I took a step in her direction to offer my help, something caught my eye. I noticed Jessie, Peyton's six-year-old cousin, stepping into place beside her. The kind-hearted youngster reached down, and, with a smile, began to fetch eggs to put in Peyton's basket. One by one the colorful eggs landed in Peyton's basket. Problem solved! Of course, this meant that Jessie couldn't gather as many for herself, but she didn't seem to mind at all. In fact, she looked perfectly happy to serve someone else, even if she had to do without.

Jessie's selfless act of kindness left a lasting impression in my mind. What a perfect biblical example she set that day. Her actions reminded me of the story of the Good Samaritan. Like Jessie, he stepped in at the perfect time, giving generously to one in need. He not only took care of the injured man, he even covered the cost. What a selfless act!

Thank you, Jessie, for the beautiful reminder that I'm called to put the needs of others before my own wants and wishes. I'll never look at another Easter basket without remembering your act of kindness.

The Closer She Gets, the Better She Looks

JANICE HANNA

"So he got up and went to his father. But while he was still a long way off, his father saw him and was filled with compassion for him; he ran to his son, threw his arms around him and kissed him."

LUKE 15:20 NIV

Remember that Clairol commercial from the 1960s—the one with the woman running across the field in slow motion? Overhead, the announcer's voice rang out: "The closer she gets, the better she looks!"

The words to that commercial run through my mind every time I see my grandchildren approaching from a distance. There's something about the way those precious toddlers greet me, especially when we haven't seen each other for a few days, that invigorates me. I hear their sweet little voices cry out, "Nina! Nina! Nina!" This would be joy enough, but seeing the look of anticipation on their precious little faces is the icing on the cake. They truly can't wait to leap into my arms, and I can't wait to plant tiny kisses all over their adorable little cheeks.

In that moment, as I lift them into the air and swing them around, my heart is on fire. To know such love is a blessing beyond anything I've ever experienced. Never have I felt so wanted, so appreciated, so at home. Never have I wanted to share my enthusiasm, my joy, or my love with anyone more deserving.

Perhaps you've experienced this same "rush" when you're around your grandchildren. If we get this excited around our grandbabies, can you even imagine what God feels like when we run into His arms? Doesn't it thrill your soul to think about how excited He must get? What joy! What peace!

God hears us calling out His name, our voices getting closer and closer as we run in His direction. And He's crying out something for us to hear, too. Can you hear Him whispering, "The closer she gets. . . the better she looks!"

How can He possibly see us this way when we're so flawed? So completely human? Easy! God doesn't see our sin, our bad behavior, or our mess-ups. He sees His kids, covered by His blood, innocent and free. We really do look good, even up close!

The next time you sweep your grandchildren into your arms, think of your heavenly Father celebrating your arrival into His presence. Contemplate His excitement. Share in His joy. Realize His eternal perspective. And take the time to pause and thank Him for seeing you as He does, washed clean by the precious blood of His Son.

To the Rescue

BETTY OST-EVERLEY

Above all, love each other deeply,
because love covers over a multitude of sins.
1 PETER 4:8 NIV

My mother was a self-described "older" mother. My parents had problems getting pregnant or staying pregnant, so when I, their first child, finally came along, mom was thirty-three years old. She handled parenthood from a much more mature perspective than many of her contemporaries, and I like to think that I benefited from that.

I, on the other hand, was twenty-six when my firstborn (and Mom's first grandchild) arrived. At the various baby showers, my mom looked at all the new-fangled paraphernalia, remarking several times, "We didn't have anything like that when you were a baby." The fact that the hospital wouldn't even allow a couple to leave without strapping the newborn into a car seat absolutely floored my mother. And, give a baby formula that was made with water straight from the tap instead of boiling it first? Sacrilege!

Despite what I "thought" I knew, my lack of experience was pretty evident within my first week of official motherhood. I soon realized what an asset my mother's maturity and know-how was going to be.

Shortly after little Rachel and I arrived home, she became fussy. She had never fussed like that in the hospital, and I assumed she was hungry. I nursed and burped her. The baby dozed off in my arms, so I put her in her crib, anxious for a little rest myself. Rachel was asleep maybe twenty-five minutes when she started crying again. I checked her diaper. It didn't seem particularly wet to me, but I changed it anyway. This time, she didn't go back to sleep easily, and I decided to use my new rocking chair. Back and forth we went. I was plenty sleepy, but sleep wasn't coming easily to Rachel.

By then the fussing had turned to screaming at the top of her lungs. I was exhausted and overwhelmed by a new little human who couldn't tell me what was wrong. I phoned my mother.

"Mom, can you come over?"

"Sure, honey. What's wrong?"

"I don't know. I've fed her, burped her, changed her diaper, and she won't hush up!"

"I'm on my way."

Fifteen minutes later, Grandma walked in to find both a crying baby and a crying new mother.

Almost immediately, the baby responded to learned hands.

"What did you do?" I asked, wiping the tears from my eyes.

"I held her confidently. But she acts colicky. Let's give her a bath. Sometimes that helps."

As I gathered the bath supplies, Mom continued to give me more little tidbits of advice. I was hesitant at first to bathe the baby, but Mom continued to encourage me and give me pointers. By the end of the bath, Rachel was much happier and so was I.

Neither my mother nor I were perfect parents. However, our deep love for our families made up for our shortcomings. In that same way, the Father's deep love also covers us. Thank God today for His great love!

The Grandma Diaries:
Edification

Grandma serves kisses, counsel, and cookies daily.

Unknown

Nana's Prize

TINA KRAUSE

Let another praise you, and not your own mouth.
PROVERBS 27:2 NIV

Alex is next. That's me hauling a camera and a bulging diaper bag. Hubby's toting the camcorder, and Jeff and Theresa are carrying the prize. . .uh, I mean the baby.

I'm pressing my way through a crowd of anxious parents and proud grandparents. Location is everything as I squeeze between other grandparents to find a strategic place from which to capture my grandson's attention with my zany faces and Garfield smiles. The other relatives are already seated. Not me—I'm too nervous. I think I'll stand.

"Make sure he gets his rest," I instructed his parents the day before our hometown's cutest baby contest. Out of 150 babies and toddlers, Alex was chosen as one of the twelve finalists. Today is the last competition. "If he's rested, he'll be his bubbly self," I decreed. Instead, his parents informed me that he took a shorter-than-usual nap. Now I'm worried.

When Alex made the finals I announced it to everyone, even strangers. "Oh," I added, "and did I tell you that last spring he placed third in another baby contest?"

When my own sons were small, I wouldn't dream of bragging about them that way, and I was intolerant of parents who did. But with my grandbaby, I'm out of control. I blather constantly about his charming gestures, cute faces, and endearing ways. Prepared and eager, I pack a wallet-size portfolio of my favorite pictures of Alex and whisk them from my purse at the mere mention of his name. "And do you know what else he does. . . ?" I query unsuspecting listeners.

The Bible instructs us not to brag about ourselves but says nothing about grandkids. So I figure that it is okay for grandparents to boast about their grandchildren; after all, it's part of our job description, right up there with spoiling. . .I mean soothing.

Uh-oh, it's Alex's turn. He's so adorable in his new outfit. I'm glad I bought several from which to choose. "Alex, Alex. Ababa-boo-boo-dada. Smile for Nana. Give Nana the 'O' face."

"Mom, remember when you spoke in articulate sentences?" daughter-in-law Theresa reminds me from behind. This, however, is no time for dignity.

"Alex, over here, baby. . ." *What's wrong? He's not his wonderful self, and the two-minute judging time is almost over.* My palms are sweating, and the butterflies in my stomach have morphed into dragonflies. "Alex baby. . .Alex sweetheart. . ." His nap. Why didn't his parents make sure he slept longer? He's not his usual self.

Alex didn't win first place, and we left the contest disappointed but undaunted. "He's still *my* winner," I chime as the hall empties. In the distance I hear similar words echo from the mouths of ten sets of other grandparents.

So we lick our wounds and climb into the car. Wait. Someone from the crowd beckons us. "Your grandson sure is cute!" My eyes widen as I pull the photo portfolio from my purse and dash across the parking lot.

"Hey, would you like to see some recent photos? You know, he usually smiles all the time, I don't know what happened today. . . ."

Okay, I admit my behavior is a tad excessive. But who else is better qualified to boast about this prize, I mean, this child?

Understanding Praise

Jo Upton

Enter into His gates with thanksgiving and a thank offering and into His courts with praise! Be thankful and say so to Him, bless and affectionately praise His name!

Psalm 100:4 AMP

Our granddaughter Leila is a joy. Since her birth two and a half years ago, we have treasured every moment we've spent with her. She is both thoughtful and playful, knowing how to get the most from every moment.

One afternoon I watched as she sat on the floor busily putting together puzzles. Her mother Tonya was in the kitchen preparing a meal to be shared by several young couples from our church that participate in a small group Bible study in their home. Since this is a gathering of families, Tonya called to Leila to let her know that her playmates would be arriving soon. Almost instantly, Leila jumped to her feet and ran toward her mother exclaiming, "Hallelujah!"

This reaction was Leila's heartfelt joy and gratitude for the knowledge that she was going to spend time with friends. No one had to prompt her to be happy—she was unable to contain what she felt and expressed it immediately!

I laughed as I watched her exuberance; her honest expression of thankfulness. To a child, words of praise come easily. But as adults, we often miss out on opportunities of praise that could result in time spent in the presence of God.

The Bible is filled with passages that encourage us to praise God, to show Him our thankfulness in all situations. In Psalm 100:4, He even tells us that our thanksgiving and praise bring us through His gates and into His courts. That's an amazing journey using only a grateful heart as a ticket!

So often in scripture it is easy to read God's advice, but we must desire to understand the importance of what He is actually asking us to do. God's request for thanksgiving isn't based on His need to *hear* it as much as it is on our need to *give* it. God understands there will be times when problems in life will threaten our faith, making it difficult to have a thankful spirit. It's at those exact moments that we need to be carried into His presence and rest in His love. If the habit of praise and thanksgiving is already part of our time with God, it will be much easier to find a reason to be grateful. Then, as we express that praise, we can be taken directly to Him to find comfort when we need it most. A thankful heart focuses on God instead of the problem, allowing room for relief.

In Leila's case, she was motivated to praise by the unexpected gift of time with her little friends. As adults, we must never lose sight of the greatest gift ever given to mankind: Jesus. If we can find only one reason to be ushered into God's presence by praise and thanksgiving, then the overwhelming love of Christ is surely reason enough for us to "bless and affectionately praise His name!"

The Queen of Malaprops

JEAN FISCHER

The words of the wise are like cattle prods—painful but helpful.
Their collected sayings are like a nail-studded stick
with which a shepherd drives the sheep.

ECCLESIASTES 12:11 NLT

Grandma Lily was the queen of malaprops. I didn't discover that until I was old enough to understand what a *malaprop* was. In the meantime, I took every word that came from her mouth as the gospel truth.

English was Grandma's second language. She had come to America from Germany when she was just sixteen years old. She spoke English fluently but not always correctly.

One hot summer day, my dad was busy in the yard digging out an old tree stump. Grandma, who lived with us, worried that he was working too hard. "Your father died of a major cardinal impaction [myocardial infarction]!" she scolded him. "If he was alive and saw what you're doing, he'd turn over in his grave!"

After Dad went fishing one day and cleaned his catch, Grandma told Mom to put the carcasses in the garden because they would *decompress* and fertilize the soil. Damp weather gave Grandma *science trouble*, and the neighbor across the street suffered from *Perkinson's disease*. She sent packages by *partial post*, and she complained about the big *popular tree* in our backyard. The list of malaprops went on and on, but no one ever corrected Grandma. That was both bad and good.

One weekend, when I was about six years old, my folks bought me a new parka. To me, it was just a coat, but Grandma called it a *parakeet*. At school on Monday, my first grade teacher asked each student to tell about something we did over the weekend.

"I got a new parakeet!" I said.

"How exciting!" said the teacher. "What color is it?"

"Red," I answered.

Davy Groves started bouncing up and down in his seat. His hand shot up. "Mrs. Davis! Mrs. Davis!"

"Yes, David."

"There ain't no such thing as a red parakeet."

"Isn't," Mrs. Davis corrected him. "Are you sure it's red?" she asked me.

"Just a minute," I told her. I went to the coatroom and came back with my new red coat. "See?"

"That isn't no parakeet!" Davy shouted.

I stood there, embarrassed, while the whole class laughed at me.

After school, Mom and I had a talk.

"Your grandmother sometimes uses the wrong words," Mom said, "but we don't correct her because she is our mother, and we respect our elders. If Grandma says a word that you don't understand, come to us, and we'll explain it to you."

I asked my parents often to explain Grandma's malaprops, and along the way, I learned something about my grandmother. Hidden among her many misplaced words were pearls of wisdom.

Job 12:12 says, "Wisdom is with the aged, and understanding in length of days" (ESV). My grandma's words were caring and wise, but it took me a while to figure that out. Do you honor your elderly parents by listening to them and treating them with respect?

Tool of Words

SHELLEY R. LEE

*"Whoever would love life and see good days must keep
their tongue from evil and their lips from deceitful speech."*
1 PETER 3:10 NIV

When little Mitch was not yet two, he had gone on a trip with Grandma and Grandpa to Florida. It would be a nice break for his mommy, who was also juggling an older and younger brother at that time, and Mitch tended to be a "pistol" in his younger years, as his great-grandfather would say.

Mitch did really well on the week-long trip except for one incident when he cried a lot for his mommy, who was fifteen hundred miles away in Ohio. The first few days had gone fine; Mitch was enjoying meeting family, playing with cousins his age, and seeing alligators at the "No Petting" Zoo with Grandma and Grandpa. He loved seeing the animals! He also loved that Grandpa loved eating ice cream, and frequently.

One evening Grandma and Grandpa planned to go to dinner with other family and friends, and they left Mitch with adult cousins whose children Mitch had gotten to know that week. But Mitch had had enough. He began to get very upset and homesick. The adult cousins thought it might be comforting for Mitch to talk to his mommy on the phone.

The conversation was mayhem! He could barely utter the words to tell his mommy he wanted to come home. He just wailed into the phone.

Mommy was teary-eyed, and later Grandma and Grandpa felt pretty awful, too. Thankfully little Mitch calmed down and, much to their relief, they discovered that careful word usage or lack of usage became very helpful. If they mentioned Mommy, or even said the word *Mommy*, Mitch would get upset. When they intentionally omitted the trigger word, he was calm. And they made it through the week like this and all the way through the flight home when toddler Mitch could be happily home with Mommy and Daddy and his brothers.

A couple years later when Mitch was four, Grandpa asked him, "Do you remember the time we took you to Florida when you were younger?" Recalling the story, Grandpa brought up the time that he was crying to go home.

Mitch looked at him with the face of one likely thinking about alligators and ice cream, and replied, "Maybe if you took me again, I'd remember."

Grandpa laughed heartily at the wit of this young boy, his little grandson, already learning careful word placement himself.

Even though this was a humorous moment of youth, it was a poignant reminder of the power of carefully used words. We can wield them for good purpose or manipulate them for selfish gain. The choice is ours.

Shine Like the Bright Stars

JANICE HANNA

In the same way, let your light shine before others,
that they may see your good deeds and glorify your Father in heaven.
MATTHEW 5:16 NIV

My daughter leads worship at our church, so she is accustomed to standing on a stage in front of several thousand people. She manages to stay calm, cool, and collected, even when the pressure's on. Her daughter Madysen loves to watch Mommy lead worship. In fact, she loves to dance and play on the stage when the service is over and the members of the congregation have gone home. Though she's only four, she has grandiose dreams of one day standing on the stage in front of a great crowd and performing. How do I know? She told me so herself!

It happened one Sunday just after church. Madysen asked if she could ride with me to the restaurant where we would all be meeting for lunch. From the car seat she made a joyous proclamation: "Nina, I want sing on the big stage like Mommy."

"That's wonderful, honey," I responded, speaking to her reflection in the rearview mirror. "I can't wait until you're old enough to do that. It's going to be so great!"

"Oh, Nina!" she added with a ripple of glee in her voice. "I want to shine like the bright stars!"

I must confess, I almost drove the car off the road as I heard her animated words. I could hardly stop laughing, in fact. As a theater director and the mother of four very theatrical daughters, I realized this youngster had tumbled into exactly the right family. Her passion to "be seen" (and admired) by the masses was definitely a family trait! So was her desire to perform in front of an audience.

Madysen's words have lingered in my mind from the time of our conversation until now, but not for the obvious reasons. I can't help but think that "shining like the bright stars" is exactly what God is calling all of us—His children—to do. No, He's not interested in seeing us garner accolades or win praise for our talents. He is, however, extremely interested in us living our lives in such a way that we shine His light before others. What does that light look like? It offers hope to the hopeless, joy to the joyless. It radiates God's kindness, goodness, and self-control. It extends grace, even when we don't feel like extending grace. In short, it is a direct reflection of His heart to those around us. And it's bright. . .not hiding under a bushel basket.

Sure, we all want to be famous. Well, many of us do. And some of us have great dreams of performing in front of large crowds, sharing our acting, singing, or dancing gifts with the masses. There's nothing wrong with that. However, we should be far more interested in shining a light on the One who is truly deserving, so that others can experience His love, His grace, and His forgiveness.

Yes, Madysen. . .the God who created us also longs for us to shine like the bright stars. Thank you so much for the reminder!

Learning to Talk Properly

MARCIA HORNOK

*Let no corrupt word proceed out of your mouth, but what is good
for necessary edification, that it may impart grace to the hearers.*
EPHESIANS 4:29 NKJV

At the age when a child's vocabulary expands daily, sixteen-month-old Ruby often repeated new words. But she surprised us one day when we were in the car together on our way to see Blair Castle in Scotland. We four adults—Ruby's parents and grandparents—were talking as Ruby sat in her car seat playing with GiGi, her stuffed giraffe.

Someone asked me a question, and I said, "Actually. . ."

That's when Ruby's little voice said, "Actually." I stopped talking and looked at her.

"Ruby, did you say 'actually'?"

"Actually," Ruby repeated.

Such a big word from a toddler amazed us.

Fast forward six months. I was back in Scotland for the arrival of

Ruby's new sister. Now Ruby was "Constant Comment," expressing herself in sentences and knowing many songs and nursery rhymes from memory. On my third day there, as she played with her toys, Ruby said, "My goodness!" I thought I heard my inflection.

I asked my daughter, "Has Ruby said that before?"

"No," she answered.

I realized that Ruby had imitated something she had heard me say. I would need to be more careful.

What Ruby wasn't learning so quickly, however, was table manners. During nearly every meal, Ruby asked for more food. Take strawberries, for example. In her highchair at the end of the table, Ruby would call out, "More strawberries."

Mom: "Say it correctly, please."

Ruby: "More strawberries PEESE!"

Mom: "May I have. . ."

Ruby: "May I—more strawberries PEESE!"

Then Ruby would get another sliced strawberry on her tray.

Speaking properly is a learned skill that takes time and practice. As we grow in our Christian life, we learn not to imitate others' bad habits but to speak graciously to those who hear us. This is easier to accomplish in the church foyer or the boss's office than in the family room at home. There I think I do not have to impress anyone and can let down my guard. But God hears all my words (and my tone of voice), knows all my thoughts, and discerns all my motives.

My conversations with my husband will either build up our relationship or corrupt it. Do I impart grace to my adult children when I speak with them? Grace means being kind even when someone doesn't deserve it. I can train myself to speak kindly to my family in much the same way Ruby learned to ask for things politely. My prayer should be, "May I have more graciousness PEESE!"

Grandma's Pearls:
Spiritual Life

We should all have one person who knows how to bless us despite the evidence. Grandmother was that person to me.

PHYLLIS THEROUX

Princesses and Crowns—
No Fairy Tale

TINA KRAUSE

Children's children are a crown to the aged.
PROVERBS 17:6 NIV

My six-year-old granddaughter, Kaitlyn, is a princess. Yes, I know, *all* granddaughters are princesses; however, mine actually *knows* she is. (Could that be because I've emphasized that fact so much?) Not only that, she thinks that I'm a princess, too. *Excuse me while I adjust my crown.*

Kaitlyn knows the name of each princess, what she wears, and her likes and dislikes. Of course, they all live in Cinderella's castle at Disney World or in her fanciful royal manor of make-believe.

Her imagination astounds me. She weaves stories like fine wool. I'd like to think she gets her creativity from her writer grandma. *Ahem, another major crown adjustment.* But I digress.

One day as she narrated another princess tale, I jotted down her story on paper. The story, appropriately entitled "The Scary Dream," described Cinderella's nightmare. Princess Bell was also a leading lady.

With the rhythm of reciting a memorized poem, Kaitlyn narrated her story saying, *"Cinderella sadly went to her room and began to cry. She cried so hard that she didn't hear a Crash! Bam! Boom! Spat! until it was too late. A white blanket showed up and a familiar voice screamed, Boo! Cinderella screamed and the princess [Bell] who scared her dropped the blanket as it fell to the floor with a soft thud."*

Kaitlyn describes characters and scenes in great detail: *"Bell peeked her eye out of the blanket with a scary apology."* Or, *"Bell took a deep breath in and out. . ."* and, *"Cinderella wasn't mad, but shook her head smiling."*

In fact, everything Kaitlyn does is detail-oriented. Tiaras must sparkle; shoes must match the outfit; colors must coordinate; stories must have a "Once upon a time" beginning and a "They lived happily ever after" ending. She is the quintessential girly girl. A real princess.

As believers, we are royalty in God's kingdom, too. The Prince of Peace has reserved crowns for princes and princesses alike. Jesus encourages us to seek and obey Him above all others. When we do, wisdom will grace our heads with the crown of splendor (Proverbs 4:8–9), and the crown of life is promised to those who love Him (James 1:12). All of these tiaras befit God's princesses, regardless of their age.

Heaven and God's Word are no fairy tale. One day the King of kings will honor true believers with a crown of righteousness (2 Timothy 4:8). Meanwhile, He honors grandmas with grandchildren, our crown and glory. And there's no need for crown adjustments with them. . .although, I might need help harnessing my halo from time to time.

The Bath That Lasts

Jo Upton

*If we confess our sins, He is faithful and righteous to
forgive us our sins and to cleanse us from all unrighteousness.*

1 John 1:9 nasb

Bedtime has always been one of my favorite times with my
grandchildren. When I am fortunate enough to have them with
me, we always spend the last few minutes together before sleep,
talking about the day and often sharing a story—either one I make up
especially for them or read from a book.

My youngest grandson, Chase, is in kindergarten now and has
always been the king of story time. He is learning to read, so he often
takes part in the routine, which includes a nightly devotion from a
child's Bible. During a recent visit, I allowed him to read first as we
shared the story of Jesus being baptized by John the Baptist. When the
paragraphs became a bit long, it was my turn to read. Chase was totally

involved, and I had his undivided attention as the story described how John lowered Jesus into the water. He loved the part where God spoke and told the world, "This is my Beloved Son, in whom I am well-pleased" (Matthew 3:17 NASB).

At the end of the devotion, I read the several review questions that allowed Chase to explain things in his own words. One question asked what had taken place between John and Jesus. Having just emerged from his own bath, squeaky and clean from the day's play, Chase was ready with an answer. Never hesitating, he explained to me that Jesus had been "bath-i-tized" by John. Through smiles, I explained to him that I had actually been saying "baptized." This opened our conversation to the whys of baptism, and the truth that Jesus—although sinless—was setting an example for us to follow. As he listened and asked questions, I kept thinking that maybe his childlike understanding, his way of relating to the story through his own experiences, had actually captured the whole essence of what God was saying.

According to 1 John 1:9, once we confess our sins, God is ready to give us our spiritual bath, washing away everything we have in our lives that separates us from Him. My grandson's bath had been provided by a loving parent that knew he needed to be washed clean, but also knew he couldn't do it without help. In a much greater way, our heavenly Father understood, even before He created the world, that He would have to provide the way for us to be rescued from the sin that would cling to us in this life.

When it seems the world just doesn't have the answers to make us happy, or to meet each need, we are finally becoming wise enough to know we need a bath. . .not with soap and water, but with the forgiving Spirit of God through our faith in what Jesus provided for us on the cross. The old hymn "Nothing But the Blood," written by Robert Lowry, clearly asks and answers the question: "What can wash away my sins? Nothing but the blood of Jesus." When we accept this spiritual cleansing, we are able to start anew, never separated from God again!

Temporary Construction Zone

Linda Holloway

*But on the judgment day, fire will reveal
what kind of work each builder has done.*

1 Corinthians 3:13 nlt

Our grandsons, Josh and Bailey, bounced from living room to sunroom to family room while they laughed and bumped each other. The unusual snowy Thanksgiving added to the excitement of the day. In addition, Uncle Kevin, home for the holidays, promised to help them build a snowman.

"Hurry, Uncle Kevin," said Josh.

"Yeah, let's go," said Bailey, as he tugged Kevin's arm.

"Okay, okay. We've got to put on our coats."

"And hats," said Tamara, Bailey's mom.

Whenever Kevin visited, it was like having three youngsters in the house. I typically hovered to remind them, "Not in the house, boys," if their roughhousing threatened furniture or the cat. As soon as the noisy group charged out the front door, the absence of chaos almost left a vacuum. . .for a few seconds.

"Come on," said Bret to his sister. "Let's throw snowballs at 'em."

"Not yet. Let's wait until they finish the snowman." She headed toward the kitchen. "Anyone for coffee?"

I sank into my swivel rocker by the picture window, exhausted from dinner, cleanup, and hyper boys. Shortly the fresh-brewed aroma filled the house, and I gratefully accepted the cup Tamara brought me.

Jerry, my husband, joined us after deboning the turkey. "That wet snow's perfect for building. Probably great for snowballs," he said.

"That's what I'm thinking," said Bret, as he carried his empty cup to the kitchen.

Tamara stepped to the window. "But we're waiting until they're through with the snowman."

Bret stared out another window. "I'm outta here." He grabbed his coat and rushed out the door.

Soon a snowman with twig arms grew in our yard. Kevin dug around in the landscape and found two rocks for eyes.

"It needs a hat," said Jerry. "Where's the Uncle Sam hat?"

"I'll check the bedroom closet."

Tamara's shout drew me back to the window like a magnet. Kevin inexplicably kicked the bottom of the snowman again and again. Jerry knocked on the glass. "What are you doing?"

"It's time to tear down this big guy," he shouted and grinned. "He's gonna melt anyway."

I watched the boys' faces. Frowns morphed into smiles. Next, each of them booted their handiwork. Then they hit it and shoved it. Bret hung back and shook his head. He glanced at us and shrugged. Then he smirked.

"Splat!" An icy missile caught Kevin's shoulder. He scooped up a handful of snow, packed together a ball, and hurled it at Bret. A fierce battle ensued, and a blizzard of snow filled the air. The only casualty was the snowman.

Our works don't have to disappear like the boys' snowman. We need materials that will last when we build on our foundation, Jesus Christ. Spending time daily in God's Word and in prayer will enable us to turn from worldly wisdom as we work through our lives.

Grandma's Dog

CONOVER SWOFFORD

Whoever does not accept the kingdom
of God like a child will never enter it.

MARK 10:15 NEB

Kelly had the unpleasant task of informing her son and daughter, Keane and Kiley, that their grandmother's dog, whom they loved, had died. The children asked plenty of questions wanting to know how and why and when. Kelly answered them as best she could. Keane decided that the dog had gone to heaven. As they were in the car going to their grandmother's house, Kelly noticed that Kiley was whispering to herself in the backseat.

"What are you doing, Kiley?" Kelly asked.

"I'm asking God to make Grandma's dog all better and send her back down here to us."

What did Jesus mean about accepting the kingdom of God like a child? Children believe God can and will do anything. As adults we might view the world a little more cynically. We may think that there is no way certain things could come to pass. God doesn't promise that they will. He does say that we can ask. And He says that all things are possible with Him. Perhaps we confuse *possible* with *probable*. God didn't say all things are probable with Him. It's not up to us to decide what is probable. God can do impossible things, and He can do things we never imagined. While it's not likely that God would send the dog back down from heaven, wouldn't we be amazed if He did? Children think anything is possible. That's the attitude that God wants us to have. He wants us to trust Him enough to know that He can do whatever He thinks is best for us.

One of the reasons God gave us our grandchildren is so that we can learn from them. If we and their parents have taught them correctly, our grandchildren will have a complete trust in God that should be inspirational to us. We should have this type of trust in God. Jesus said that if we ask anything of the Father that is in accordance with His will, we shall have it. Learning to trust God more helps us to know Him more. The more we know Him, the more we know what His will is for us. Then we pray, asking for things we know He wills us to have and we trust Him to give them to us.

The best way to handle any problem is to ask God to take care of it and then trust Him to do it. We don't need to tell Him how we think He should handle it. We don't need to lean unto our own understanding. God's ways are not our ways. He thinks of things we've never even imagined. His solutions to our problems will usually be something we never ever thought of. God is much more creative than we are.

The more we love God, the more we trust Him. We're never too old to have a childlike spirit.

I Didn't Ask You

CONOVER SWOFFORD

Then I heard a loud voice saying in heaven, "Now salvation,
and strength, and the kingdom of our God, and the power
of His Christ have come, for the accuser of our brethren,
who accused them before our God day and night, has been cast down."
REVELATION 12:10 NKJV

Nita's son Robert and his family were visiting her for the Thanksgiving holidays. On Thanksgiving morning, Nita's four-year-old granddaughter Bonnie came into the kitchen yawning and stretching.

"Grandma," Bonnie said, "can I have ice cream for breakfast?"

Before Nita could reply, Robert said to his daughter, "Sweetheart, we don't eat ice cream for breakfast."

Bonnie looked at her father and said, "I didn't ask you."

Nita grinned at her son and got Bonnie some ice cream for breakfast.

In our spiritual battle, Satan can tempt us to despair because we know that we are guilty of what he is accusing us of. We look at our failures and our sins and wonder how God could possibly forgive us one more time. Satan wants us to feel hopeless, like we can never measure up. The truth is that we can't measure up. It's impossible. But we don't have to measure up. Satan can accuse us all he wants. God simply smiles and says, "Not guilty. The price has been paid." Because of Jesus' finished work on Calvary, God's grace covers us. So if we hear a little voice telling us, "You are doomed," we can say, "I didn't ask you." We don't have to listen to anything negative about ourselves. God sees us as perfect because we are in Christ and God only sees Him.

But sometimes we forget that. We see all our flaws and weaknesses. That's when we need to realize that we are focusing on the wrong thing. God doesn't focus on our flaws and weaknesses. In fact He is busy loving us and blessing us. The more Satan accuses us, the more we need to turn to God and to follow Jesus' example. When Satan tried to tempt Jesus, Jesus answered him with scripture. Satan tries to tell us we're not good enough to be blessed, that God couldn't possibly want anything to do with us. He tries to get us to feel condemned. And he might succeed. But if we feel condemned, all we have to do is turn to Romans 8:1, which says there is no condemnation to us who are in Christ Jesus and who are walking according to His Spirit. In fact, we can read all of Romans 8, which explains how much God loves us and how absolutely nothing can separate us from His love.

Any time a negative thought makes us feel bad about ourselves, we can simply say to our accuser, "I didn't ask you." Instead we turn to our Father and ask Him to cleanse us from all unrighteousness. Then we trust Him to fight our battles for us.

Shut Up, I'm Praying

CONOVER SWOFFORD

*"And when you pray, do not be like the hypocrites, for they love to pray
standing in the synagogues and on the street corners to be seen by others.
Truly I tell you, they have received their reward in full."*

MATTHEW 6:5 NIV

Marie had her two grandsons at her house for dinner. As they
sat down at the table, Marie's older grandson, George, was all
excited. He had learned a new grace that day at preschool and wanted to
say the blessing. As George began to sing the little song he had learned,
his little brother Hal started singing, too. George stopped singing
and said, "Shut up, Hal! I'm praying!"

Marie said gently, "George, Hal can pray with you if he wants to."

"But it's my prayer," George protested.

This is what was happening at the church in Corinth. They had
gotten so full of themselves and their own spiritual gifts that instead of

using them to edify each other, they were using them as competition. We might laugh at George's reaction, but we must be careful that we don't have that attitude when we pray. Prayer isn't about the words we are saying. It's not a competition as to who can say the better prayer. Prayer is about the intent of our hearts.

Some people think of prayer as a thing in and of itself. They are more concerned with their phrasing and the way it sounds than with the fact that they are actually talking to God. They write down a prayer so they can get it right. Perhaps they are giving a prayer in church or in front of some group and they are concerned with what people will think of how they pray. Prayer isn't about impressing other people.

When the Pharisee and the tax collector went into the temple to pray, the Pharisee's "prayer" was really a list of all his accomplishments. He wasn't just trying to impress those around him, he was trying to impress God. As Jesus said in the verse above, the Pharisee had all the reward he was going to get. But the prayer that impressed God was the tax collector's prayer, "God be merciful to me, a sinner."

We don't want to abuse the privilege of prayer. We want to use it to glorify our Father in heaven. When he was on Mount Carmel with the prophets of Baal, Elijah prayed that God would send the fire he asked for so that the people would know that God was God and that Elijah was His servant. Elijah's prayer was answered because he prayed for the right thing. He wasn't praying for God to send fire so that all the people would be impressed with him, Elijah, but so that they would be impressed with God. God not only hears every word we say, He knows the intent of our hearts. We can't pray effectively if we're only saying words and trying to impress others.

Beyond the Looking Glass

JO UPTON

For now we see only a reflection as in a mirror;
then we shall see face to face. Now I know in part;
then I shall know fully, even as I am fully known.
1 CORINTHIANS 13:12 NIV

We recently attended the high school graduation of my oldest granddaughter, Brittany. She is a wonderful, intelligent young woman whose relationship with Christ influences all her decisions. As I sat there watching the beautiful ceremony, I couldn't help but recall memories from her childhood; in particular, things that she and I had shared. One specific incident stuck in my head: "The window performance."

Brittany had been allowed to spend the night at our house, and we were making the most of every moment. Our final project was to bake cookies, something we loved to do together. As we waited for them to come from the oven, Brittany looked around for something else to do. After rummaging through a box of toys, she settled on a large cowboy hat. I continued to work in the kitchen until movement from the dining area caught my attention. Apparently the hat had inspired a song and dance reenactment of a local TV commercial. With the hat perched on her head, she pranced back and forth in front of the large, uncovered windows. With night as a backdrop, her reflection in the windows was almost as sharp as if she had been dancing in front of mirrors. The trees in the backyard provided shelter from neighboring houses, so she gave it her all, watching with joy as her reflection mimicked every move. She thought her routine was being performed in total privacy, but her security was false. As I stood in the kitchen, partially hidden by cabinets, she never suspected that I could see everything. She could only see from her side of the room, so she wasn't aware that the same reflection providing her personal entertainment was also showcasing each movement for me.

Sometimes we behave the same way. We think we have all the information, facts, and wisdom needed to move through life successfully. If we aren't careful, we spend each day of a lifetime performing for ourselves, not fully understanding that we have only a partial picture. If we truly understood the importance of our lives, fully knew what God intended for us, we would surely live with a different perspective and purpose.

There is so much more to our relationship with God than we could ever know on this side of the "mirror." We don't understand how everything works from our earthly view, seldom grasping the grander plan. But with the knowledge we do have, we must trust that someday God—who knows us completely—will allow us to know Him in the same way. As the scripture explains, someday we will understand everything, realizing just how much God loved us through His Son. Then, with a completed picture, we can continue to praise the God who so generously provided it all!

Letting God Be God

MARCIA HORNOK

"Who has known the mind of the Lord? Or who has been his counselor?
Who has ever given to God, that God should repay them?"
ROMANS 11:34–35 NIV

W hy did Mommy and Daddy go away?" five-year-old Lauren asked. I was caring for Lauren and her three-year-old sister while their parents took a trip to celebrate their anniversary. Driving home from church with the two girls in their car seats, I considered Lauren's plaintive question.

"Mommy and Daddy will come back, honey," I answered. "They just want to have a vacation together. In three days they will be home again."

"Why did they go?" she asked again.

"Because they love each other. They want to be together and do some fun things."

Then Lauren said, "Well, they better not get married!"

I was laughing too hard to ask what she had against marriage or to inform her that her comment was nine years too late. She obviously had a disconnect in her thinking.

Many times I think like a five-year-old with my Father God. He seems to have gone away and left me on my own. I wonder where He is and why He has deserted me when I need Him most. Erroneously I think that He should do what I expect. Sometimes I even have the attitude: "I know He loves me, but He better not mess with my life."

Too late for that! Not only is He my Creator and Savior, and thus has a "right" to my life, but I have also surrendered my life to Him for His glory. Trouble is, I have my own ideas of what "for His glory" should mean. I think He should answer my prayers a certain way because that would give me the best possible results, or He should improve my health so I can be more productive, or He should heal my child's marriage because He hates divorce (Malachi 2:16).

If I'm honest, it's really "my glory" that would benefit. Since God will not give His glory to another, He must deal with me His way. What He can do *in* me is more important to Him than what He can do *with* me. Someone has said that God is more concerned with our character than our comfort. Thus He will do devastating things to me that I cannot figure out, because I need to learn to trust in Him and not in myself as 2 Corinthians 1:9 states. I am merely a worker in His vineyard, and He has a right to do what He wants with what belongs to Him (Matthew 20:15).

Lauren had her mistaken idea about what her parents should do or not do. I need to make sure that I do not set a precedent about how my Father God should deal with me. He alone is God! I don't have to know what He's doing in my life, because He does.

Fig Leaf Efforts

Marcia Hornok

Not having my own righteousness, which is from the law, but that which is through faith in Christ, the righteousness which is from God by faith.
Philippians 3:9 NKJV

Phineas raced across the living room as fast as his hands and knees could carry him. At ten months, he was interacting with his surroundings more every day. So when his sock slipped off one foot during his speed crawl, he kept going for about two yards, then stopped. We could almost see his mind processing that something had changed.

He pushed to a sitting position and looked back to where he had come from. Spotting his sock on the carpet, he crawled back to it, then sat up again.

Picking up his sock, he laid it on top of his bare foot. And that was that. Phineas had experienced a problem and tried his best to fix it but had failed. He had no ability to solve the case of the naked foot.

Phineas's dilemma portrays everyone's; a problem that goes all the way back to our first parents. Adam and Eve lost their innocence when they ate the forbidden fruit. Suddenly they realized something had changed. Their nakedness now brought shame, so they sewed together fig leaves and tried to dress themselves. These sticky, somewhat prickly leaves may have covered their bodies, but could not cover their sin or forgive their offense. For that, God had to provide the solution.

He made clothing out of animal skins (Genesis 3:21). Thus animal sacrifice entered the human experience and culminated in the human sacrifice of Christ, the Lamb of God, as payment in full for the sin of the world (John 1:29). God had warned Adam and Eve that they would "surely die" when they disobeyed Him. They died spiritually and began to die physically when they ate from the tree. To fix that problem, Jesus died spiritually and physically on the cross. That's why He alone guarantees eternal life to all who trust in Him for it.

How relieved I am that my relationship with God does not depend upon my own ingenuity or ability. In fact, Isaiah 1:18 compares my righteous acts to "filthy rags." My sin debt can only be fixed by having the righteousness of Christ put on my account. "To the one who does not work but trusts God who justifies the ungodly, their faith is credited as righteousness" (Romans 4:5 NIV). Yes, God is the only one who can fix our sin problem, and we can take all our other problems to Him as well. A popular hymn says, "Take your burden to the Lord and leave it there."

Eventually Phineas had to let his mom put the sock on his foot. In much the same way, we must let Jesus Christ put us right with God by depending on the work He has done for us, not on what we try to do for Him.

Lily and the Crackernut

MARCIA HORNOK

I sought the LORD, and He heard me,
and delivered me from all my fears.
PSALM 34:4 NKJV

I asked my four-year-old granddaughter what she wanted for Christmas. Without hesitation she answered, "A crackernut."

"You want crackers with nuts in them?"

"No," she giggled.

"Do you mean nuts that you can crack open?"

"No, Grandma, a toy—like Clara's crackernut."

The story of Clara Stahlbaum falling asleep under the Christmas tree while holding the nutcracker Godfather Drosselmeyer had given her had captured Lily's heart. She wanted a nutcracker of her own. I asked her why.

"To play with." Then she thought some more and added, "And if a rat comes in my room at night, the crackernut will chase him away."

Lily and her brother Xander were our step-grandkids. They had experienced lots of changes in their preschool years, including having a new set of grandparents in their lives. They cried when they had to leave their mother; they cried when they had to leave their dad; so when they spent the night in our home, I taught them a song to help overcome their fears:

"When I feel afraid, I will trust in God. He is with me all the time—I will trust in God," sung to the tune of "Row, Row, Row Your Boat." We substituted other words in the first line to fit whatever they feared: When the thunder sounds. . . When it's dark outside. . . When I'm all alone. . .

But children aren't the only ones with fears. Often I'm afraid God won't take care of me or work out a bad situation the way I want Him to. So I take matters into my own hands by buying something I cannot afford, indulging in empty calories, or calling up a friend instead of praying. Many times I depend on self-help books, how-to articles, or Internet searches rather than on the scriptures for comfort, wisdom, and guidance. When I put my trust in other things besides God, it's a matter of fear.

I'm afraid the money will run out, my children will make bad decisions, I'll get ill and become a burden, or my body will outlive my mind.

I need to remember the words I wrote: *He is with me all the time. I will trust in God.* For all my circumstances and losses, "He Himself has said, 'I will never leave you nor forsake you.' So we may boldly say: " 'The Lord is my helper; I will not fear' " (Hebrews 13:5–6 NKJV).

Lily turned nine this year. She still gets a nutcracker every Christmas and now has a nice collection. Recently I asked her about them: "Do you still think your crackernuts can protect you at night?"

To my relief she answered, "Not really. God does that."

Maybe someday I'll remember that, too!

911:
What Is Your Emergency?

BETTY OST-EVERLEY

I call upon the LORD, who is worthy to
be praised, and I am saved from my enemies.
PSALM 18:3 NASB

As a single parent, I was very thankful that my mother was my backup babysitter.

Because I was the sole breadwinner for my little family, I couldn't take off work every time there was a snow day at school, or one of the kids had the sniffles or was feverish. Grandma was always willing to sit, and the kids received her tender loving care.

One day I dropped off both Rachel and Jacob at Grandma's house on my way to work. The schools had closed due to snow and subzero temperatures, and I was preparing myself for a terrible drive to work.

At least I didn't have to worry about my children.

"Call me if you need anything, Mom," I said as I rushed out the door.

My kindergarten-aged son, Jacob, was mesmerized by anything with push buttons. These objects would keep him entertained for hours. Jake's first stop this morning was Grandma's toy box, where he dug out his favorite broken calculator to play with.

Meanwhile, Grandma made hot cocoa for both the kids and switched on an educational program on the television set for Rachel, who was busy with a coloring book. The kids were happy and quiet, and Grandma started a little housework.

Mom says she was gone for only a minute. She went to her upstairs bedroom for an item, and as she was descending the steps, she saw that Jake had the telephone receiver up to his ear.

"Put that down, Jacob!"

Jake promptly returned the telephone handset to the cradle.

"What were you doing, Jake?" Grandma inquired.

"Nothing, Grandma."

As she passed the desk, the phone rang.

"Hello."

"Mrs. Topping, this is 911. Do you have an emergency there?"

"No. Why would you think that?"

"Because we just received a hang-up call from your number."

Grandma glared at Jake.

"No, everything is just fine. Thank you for calling."

Mom took Jake by the hand, leading him to the couch, where she picked him up and put him on her lap. She was going to have a little talk with the young man.

"Why did you do that, Jake? Was it because the phone has push buttons on it?"

Jake pointed to the television. "Sesame Street."

Mom frowned, not understanding.

"What about Sesame Street?"

"They were talking about 911 on Sesame Street today, Grandma."

Rachel's information completed the missing puzzle piece. Jake had quickly learned that 911 was an important number to know.

You might not realize it, but you have your own 911 emergency system. All you need to do is call on God in prayer. God promises His full attention and a loving answer to our prayers. Don't hesitate to call on the Lord. . .any time!

All-Seeing Eyes

Jo Upton

*"If anyone causes one of these little ones—those who believe in me—
to stumble, it would be better for them if a large millstone were
hung around their neck and they were thrown into the sea."*
MARK 9:42 NIV

Before my oldest grandson, Jonathan, started going to school, he would often attend church services with his family. He loved the music and singing; in particular, one young man that played the bongos. Whenever a song or musical special called for bongos, Jonathan was enthralled, hardly moving a muscle. Watching the enthusiasm with which this young man performed eventually resulted in Jon asking for a set of bongos to play. He was truly a fan. But then something happened that took his admiration to a whole new level.

One day, while shopping with his mother and me at a large toy store, Jon spotted the young man. With eyes of wonder, he discovered that this man not only played bongos, he also worked at the most wonderful place on earth—a toy store! Jon pleaded with his mom to let him talk to the "church man," so she approached him and explained the whole story, beginning with the bongos. The man smiled and graciously shook Jon's tiny hand. After a few minutes of conversation, we left. This previously unknown man, without changing one thing in his life, had made a profound impact on my small grandson.

I've thought about that chance meeting at the toy store. We didn't set out to meet this man, or to have Jon see him at work. It just happened. How wonderful that Jon was able to see him doing a worthwhile job and displaying an attitude of friendliness. How different it might have been if we had seen him involved in something that didn't reflect Christian character. I'm sure Jon would have been hurt and confused if he had seen this man doing something that he knew to be wrong.

Jesus didn't pull any punches when He described the consequences for those who cause others to stumble in their faith, especially "little ones." Parents, grandparents, teachers—anyone who associates with younger children or those new to their faith—need to take their roles very seriously. Our lives are in the spotlight and we have to measure up. Perfection isn't necessary, or even obtainable, but a life that focuses on God is certainly within reach. Living by God's values and instructions makes all the difference in how things turn out for us as well as those watching. And, as the young man in the band discovered, sometimes you're unaware that you're being watched until you've already made that important first impression.

As grandparents, there are many times when we have the opportunity to influence our grandchildren. Sometimes it's with words of advice, but always with the things they see us doing. The daily choices we make, although seemingly small at the time, can ultimately attract or repel our grandchildren from the faith we profess. What a wonderful privilege to know that by living the life God designed for us, we are also helping to shape the lives of those we love the most!

Grandma's Medicine:
Laughter

What children need most are the essentials that grandparents provide in abundance. They give unconditional love, kindness, patience, humor, comfort, lessons in life. And, most importantly, cookies.

Rudolph Giuliani

Give Up and Laugh!

LINDA HOLLOWAY

A cheerful heart is good medicine.
PROVERBS 17:22 NIV

Our two grandsons, ages six and ten, disrupted our family Christmas dinner several times. Bailey and Josh giggled during the prayer, complained about the food, and clamored to leave the table early. We wanted to visit with our adult son and daughter but almost gave up.

"Settle down!" said Bret, Josh's dad.

Tamara, Bailey's mother, reminded them, "No presents until after dinner."

"Okay," they said in unison.

We adults chatted for five peaceful minutes. Then Grandpa Jerry said, "Let's do the present thing."

Of course, the gift exchange was noisy, exciting, and short. The men picked up the colorful paper and organized the presents into six piles.

After a brief rest, Tamara and I retreated to the kitchen to clean up the dinner dishes. "It's pretty quiet out there," I said as we dried our hands.

"Yeah. What's wrong?"

"We'd better see why they're so quiet." We walked toward the living room. The sight stopped us in our tracks. The two cousins sat together in the swivel rocker, talking in low voices.

"Aren't they adorable?" whispered Tamara.

I nodded. We tiptoed closer for a better view. Josh held the Christmas video tape as he and Bailey chatted about the characters pictured on its cover. Tamara and I smiled and sighed.

Shortly, Bret plodded down the stairs. "What's up?" he said to no one in particular.

Simultaneously Tamara and I put our index fingers to our mouths. "Shh."

When he glanced our way, we grinned and pointed to the boys. He studied them for a moment and then crept toward the pair. Suddenly, he grabbed their chair and spun it. *Whish!* They whooped and spilled to the floor. Laughter filled the air as they lunged at Bret. The three wrestled and rolled around the floor. So much for the dinner afterglow.

Unable to calculate where the tangle of arms, legs, and heads would tumble next, I stood rooted to the floor. "Watch out for the tree!" I yelled.

"Couldn't help yourself, huh?" said Tamara to Bret.

He raised his head like a periscope and peered at her. "Nope," he said just before the boys tugged him back into their clutches.

She and I frowned at him. Unable to hold our stern expressions, we burst into riotous laughter.

"What's going on?" said Jerry, descending the steps. Quiet fell over the room. The three on the floor stopped and stared at him.

No answer. . .from anyone. He scanned each frozen face. Soon guffaws engulfed us all.

That Christmas afternoon I learned to relax and enjoy the comical scene that unfolded. Instead of trying to control it, I gave up and laughed.

Praise the Lord for the gift of laughter to smooth out the rough edges of family life. Whenever the opportunity presents itself, we do well to laugh together. Seeing humor in a situation not only eases tension, but also creates lasting memories.

Happy News

CONOVER SWOFFORD

And the Lord blessed the latter days of Job more than his beginning.
JOB 42:12 AMP

Margaret was having a difficult day. Her refrigerator was leaking water all over the kitchen floor. Her sister Dottie had called to say she was ill and needed some help. Her Boston bull terrier Sammy got loose from the yard and she had to chase him all over the neighborhood. By the time Margaret caught Sammy and got him back to the house, she was tired, sweaty, and more than a little outdone. As she came into her kitchen, the phone rang. Margaret said out loud to herself, "This had better not be any more bad news. I need some happy news."

Her grandson Hayden smiled at her and said, "I have happy news. I'm smart, Gran."

Margaret couldn't help but smile at him and that smile lifted her spirits.

Some days we may feel like Job—like everything that can go wrong has gone wrong. We all need happy news, and we can have it. In Colossians 1:27, Paul says we have Christ in us, the hope of glory. What is our hope of glory? John says it is that we will see Jesus and become just like Him. No matter what goes wrong, we have our sights on Jesus and our heavenly home. We know that for us, this world is the worst that it gets. All our good news is yet to come. Like Job, our latter days will be so much more blessed than our beginnings. In the beginning, Job had everything taken away from him at once. The Bible says that while one servant was still delivering bad news, the next servant was already coming to give more bad news. But in the end, God gave Job back twice as much as Job had lost in the beginning. His flocks and herds were doubled. That was great for Job, we might think, but how do we know that our latter days will be better than our beginnings?

God sent us His Holy Spirit to encourage and comfort us. The Bible says that the Holy Spirit is our earnest. In the days that the King James Bible was written, the word *earnest* meant the token one gave to their betrothed. Today, it would be an engagement ring. We are the Bride of Christ, and the Holy Spirit has been given to us as a pledge of Jesus' love for us. Happy news indeed! And God wants us to share our happy news with others, to give them the same hope we have—the hope of glory. Jesus gives us hope so that we can share that hope with others.

Let's show our grandchildren what living in hope means. Let's share with them our happy news, which is also their happy news. Our hope lifts our spirits and makes it easier for us to live in this world while we wait on better things to come.

I Scream, You Scream, We All Scream for Ice Cream

JANICE HANNA

Is there no balm in Gilead; is there no physician there?
why then is not the health of the daughter of my people recovered?
JEREMIAH 8:22 KJV

Several months ago, my two-and-a-half-year-old granddaughter, Peyton, asked for ice cream. As I filled her bowl, I sang a little ditty I'd learned as a kid: "I scream, you scream, we all scream for ice cream!" She loved it, and the little song stuck. Every time she wanted ice cream, the melody and lyrics rang out again. We sang it at home, in restaurants, and at ice cream parlors. Talk about fun (and talk about drawing attention to our family)!

Unfortunately, Peyton was involved in a terrible accident just a couple of months before her third birthday. She tripped and fell into a campfire. She caught herself with her hand, which sustained major burns. Because of the severity of the injury, she was transported by ambulance to a local burn center, where she remained for several days. My heart broke as I watched her go through all of this.

On a particularly rough day at the hospital, we did everything we could to console Peyton, but she was inconsolable. Through her tears, she tried to explain her pain level. In spite of heavy-duty pain meds, she still suffered terribly. My heart absolutely broke in two as I heard her cries. Still, what could I do? Sure, I prayed 'round the clock, but I wanted to be able to do something tangible. . .something she would notice.

The nurse came into the room and decided to offer Peyton the ultimate bribe to shift her attentions. . .ice cream.

I'll never forget Peyton's reaction. With tears streaming, she looked up at me and squeaked out, "I scream, you scream, we all scream for ice cream." Then she gave me a teensy-tiny smile—one that broke the tension in the room and made me laugh. Before long, we were all laughing, even our little patient. Her funny little song broke the spell of sadness. The nurse brought her a container of ice cream, which Peyton consumed with a smile.

That little song has become our ice cream motto. We can't dive into a bowl of the icy-cold, gooey goodness without singing the little tune first. It reminds us of the soothing, healing power of our favorite dessert. In many ways, it also reminds me of today's scripture about the balm of Gilead. A balm is an ointment, something that soothes. . . just like that ice cream.

God knows just what we need when we're hurting, doesn't He? Sometimes it's ice cream. Other times, it's a kind word from a friend. Often it's just a quiet moment in His presence, where He reassures us of His love.

When was the last time you interrupted life's sadness with a funny little song? It might be just the "balm" you need to soothe your troubled soul!

Cradle Robbers and the Women Who Love Them

Valorie Quesenberry

Rejoice with the wife of your youth.
Proverbs 5:18 nkjv

Both of my grandfathers were cradle robbers! No, they weren't baby snatchers; they both had very young brides. And my grandmothers had interesting tales about their induction into matrimonial bliss!

My paternal grandparents, James and Thelma, met in an old-time tent meeting. My grandfather was a young preacher, traveling in an evangelistic circuit. My grandmother and her brother were musicians, playing guitar and accordion and singing for church services. One September evening in 1935, God put them in the same town. That night, Thelma was playing the guitar, and during the song, she dropped her guitar pick. Seated on the platform, James had already decided he was interested in this young lady and seized the opportunity presented him. He clapped his foot over the pick and then later put it into his pocket so he could return it to her and meet her in the process. I don't know exactly what he said to her that night when the meeting was over, but it must have worked. James and Thelma were married two weeks later and spent fifty-nine years side by side, ministering together until his death. What is especially interesting is that my grandmother was engaged to another man the night she met my grandfather and was all of eighteen years old on her wedding day!

My maternal grandparents, Harold and Lorraine, met in a city park in St. Louis, Missouri. My grandfather and his army buddies were walking with their girlfriends through the park. My grandmother and her friend were riding rented bicycles along the same path. When their ways met, Harold asked Lorraine if he could ride her bike. She replied that it would "make his girl mad" and rode off. Strangely enough, they met up again a short while later and this time, Harold was alone! So, he got his ride and a new girl! After a whirlwind wartime romance, Harold and Lorraine were married in August 1942—she was just sixteen. They spent the next sixty-one years together.

I find a bit of humor in the fact that both my grandfathers had a funny streak in them, and it showed up in the way they met their future wives. Who could have guessed that mundane stuff like guitar picks and bicycles could become important props in a romantic tale? But, put those items into the hands of cradle robbers and they claim victory!

My grandmothers didn't always laugh their way through marriage; no, real life isn't scripted that way. But I was privileged to hear their stories told with warmth and joy. They left me a legacy of love sprinkled with good, hearty chuckles. And I think, even in old age, their eyes still twinkled when they talked about the cradle robbers with whom they had spent their lives—those sweet old rogues!

Shaking It Up

BETTY OST-EVERLEY

Greet each other in Christian love.
ROMANS 16:16 NLT

W hat's my name?" my mother asked her grandson.

My eighteen-month-old son mumbled something. Whatever it was, it didn't sound like "Grandma."

"Jacob, who is this?" I pointed to my mother.

Again, something unintelligible came from his lips.

I knew my son was having difficulty with words. He had experienced several strep infections in his young life, which led to his trying to talk with a sore throat. Jacob couldn't always close the soft palate at the back of his throat, which sometimes made his words incoherent.

"Here, let's try this," said my mother. Grabbing Jacob's hand, she pumped it up and down in a shaking motion. "Hello, I'm Grandma. What's your name?"

Jacob laughed loudly.

"Jacob!"

"That's right. Now you try it."

Jacob grabbed Grandma's hand. "Hello, my name is Jacob. What's your name?"

"Grandma!"

Everyone laughed.

For weeks afterward, every time we went to my mother's house, Jacob would extend his hand and say, "Hello, I'm Jacob. What's your name?"

The repetition paid off. Jacob was getting better about saying Grandma's name in a way that was understandable. We all thought the handshaking business was cute.

Until one morning, when my mother thought she'd die of embarrassment.

Jacob awoke not feeling particularly well, and since I had to go to work, I dropped him off at my mom's, our favorite back-up sitter. After listening to his symptoms, my mother concluded that she would need to pick up bananas and applesauce, which would help Jacob get over whatever was ailing him.

Putting him in the seat of the shopping cart, Grandma rolled Jacob through the store. While she was there, she'd pick up a few other items as well. Parking the cart within close line-of-sight, she was engrossed in reading a can label when she heard, "Hello, my name is Jacob. What's yours?"

Mom's head shot up to see an elderly couple shaking hands with her grandson.

"Jacob, it's time we leave these good people alone, okay?" as she quickly rolled the cart closer to her location. However, that didn't stop Jacob. As soon as the next person came down the aisle, he again introduced himself.

"Hello, my name is Jacob. What's yours?"

He must have introduced himself fifty times before they left the store. If it hadn't resulted in him speaking her name more clearly, Grandma would have regretted teaching him anything about shaking hands.

I think Jacob can teach us a lesson in brotherly love. In a world where people complain that we've lost certain niceties, we can help restore some of that. Strive to greet others, even strangers, in a manner that is warm and affectionate. A cheerful "hello" might be just the gift that will make someone's day.

The Fun Goes On

ARDYTHE KOLB

A cheerful heart is good medicine,
but a broken spirit saps a person's strength.
PROVERBS 17:22 NLT

When my older brother was born, Dad's mother announced, "I want Billy to call me *Grandmother*." She was used to getting her way and liked to think she was a bit sophisticated. Her husband thought "Grandfather" sounded too formal. He opted to be Granddad.

Mom's mother said, "Well, so the baby knows who's who, I'll be Grandmamma and Daddy can be Grandpapa."

By the time I came along, the titles were embedded in our family. I was eight or nine years old before I realized that some people don't have a grandmother, granddad, grandmamma, and grandpapa.

Grandmamma was tiny and spunky. Her laughter filled the air and never failed to make me happy. We lived about one hundred miles away, and besides occasional weekend trips, I was invited to spend a few days with them each summer during my growing-up years.

Grandmamma timed those visits when the carnival came to town. We would wander along the midway and try to win stuffed animals or glittery jewelry at every booth. She loved the rides and lights and music as much as any kid. When air puffed our skirts from below she'd exclaim, "Oh my! What happened?" as though she was totally shocked. Our images in wavy mirrors made her point at me and say, "You look weird! Who do you belong to?" And rooms set on a tilt left her hanging on as though she were about to tumble. Everything seemed like a new experience for her. It was no surprise that she thought cotton candy, popcorn, and snow cones were absolute necessities.

During our visits, Grandmamma taught me the basics of ballroom dancing. Giggles flooded the house as we whirled and dipped through her living room.

Saturday evenings we'd walk the three blocks to the town square and sit on the lawn of the courthouse while the local band played their weekly concert. A few couples danced in the street, and Grandmamma took my hand and led me through the routines we had practiced in her living room.

My parents sometimes got exasperated with her. "She acts like such a child!" When I overheard that, I said, "Is there something wrong with being a child?" My folks were much too serious in my young mind—children knew how to have fun.

As I grew older I understood their frustrations. Grandmamma's solution to most any problem was laughter, which was perfect as far as I could see as a child. But she could be selfish and expected others to deal with the vital parts of life, like finances, house maintenance, and even her own health care.

God probably created us to balance responsibility with enjoyment, and He gives each of us work to accomplish. But perhaps Grandmamma's purpose in life was to bring joy into her part of the world and help people find more to laugh about. If so, she accomplished her mission with pizzazz.

Contributors

When she's not laughing at her husband's antics or running scared from his newest idea, **Kathy Douglas** enjoys leading women's Bible studies at her church, spoiling her four grandsons, in-line skating—and (rarely) target shooting. You can read her blog at http://www.katherine-kathy-douglas.blogspot.com or find a listing of all her books on her website, www.katherinedouglas.com.

Jean Fischer has been writing for nearly three decades and has worked as an editor with Golden Books. She has co-written with Thomas Kinkade and John MacArthur, and is one of the authors for Barbour's Camp Club Girls series. Recent books include the *Kids' Bible Dictionary* and *199 Bible People, Places, and Things*.

Janice Hanna (who also writes as Janice Thompson) is the author of over fifty books for the Christian market. Janice lives in Spring, Texas, near her children and grandchildren. She spends her days writing, teaching, and speaking.

Bestselling and award-winning author **Anita Higman** has twenty-six books published (several coauthored) for adults and children and has seven more books coming out. She's been a Barnes & Noble "Author of the Month" for Houston and has a BA degree, combining communication, psychology, and art. Please visit her site at www.anitahigman.com.

Linda Holloway is a freelance writer, speaker, and teacher. She's written devotions and magazine articles and also contributed nonfiction stories to several collections. She teaches a creative writing class, Bible studies, and women's retreat sessions. Linda and her husband Jerry live in Prairie Village, Kansas, near their two almost-grown grandsons.

Marcia Hornok, managing editor of *CHERA Fellowship* magazine, raised her six children in Utah, where her husband pastors Midvalley Bible Church. She loves interacting with grandkids, cooking Sunday dinners for her family, partnering with her husband in ministry, and playing Spider Solitaire. She has contributed devotionals to seven other books.

Ardythe Kolb has written stories, articles, and devotions for multiple publications and is currently working on two books. She and her husband owned a Christian bookstore while they raised their family. They live in eastern Kansas, near children, grandchildren, and great-grandbabies. She enjoys family, friends, writing, volunteer work, and travel.

Tina Krause is the author of *Laughter Therapy* and Barbour's *Grand Moments for Grandmothers*, *The Bible Promise Book for Women*, *Life Is Sweet*, and *God's Answers for Your Life—Parents' Edition*. She is a contributor to over twenty book compilations and has nine hundred published writing credits. A freelance writer and award-winning newspaper columnist, Tina lives with her husband Jim in Valparaiso, Indiana, where they enjoy spoiling their five grandchildren.

Shelley R. Lee has authored numerous articles, two books, and contributed to five others, most recently *Heavenly Humor for the*

Dieter's Soul (Barbour Publishing); and she is the editorial manager for WhatAVisit.com. She grew up in Michigan and earned her bachelor's degree at Grand Valley State University where she met her husband of twenty-five years, David. They reside in rural northwest Ohio with their four teen- and college-age sons, and never enough groceries. Shelley posts humorous stories regularly at www.shelleyrlee.blogspot.com.

Betty Ost-Everley is married to Terry, is the mother of two, and lives in Kansas City, Missouri. When not working as an administrative assistant or changing her neighborhood as a community activist, Betty is an advisory board member of the Heart of America Christian Writers' Network.

Valorie Quesenberry is a pastor's wife, mother of four, blogger, speaker, and writer. She is the author of two books, *Reflecting Beauty: Embracing the Creator's Design* (Wesleyan Publishing House, 2010) and Redeeming Romance: Delighting in God's Love. Valorie enjoys communicating truth through both fiction and nonfiction.

Conover Swofford resides in Columbus, Georgia. A freelance writer for over twenty-five years, Conover enjoys reading and participates in many of her church's community activities.

Jo Upton has been writing for more than twenty years from her desk in Georgia. Three of her five grandchildren live nearby. In a perfect world, all five would be living upstairs, just waiting to say something wonderful she could put into print!

Scripture Index